NOT TAKING A FENCE

Verses, Stories, and Memories from the Heart of Appalachia

Volume I: From Contemporary Poems to Grave Robbing and Home Wakes

Collected and Edited by Danny R. Kuhn

Favoritetrainers.com Books
Myrtle Beach, South Carolina

Not Taking a Fence
Verses, Stories, and Memories from the Heart of Appalachia
Volume I: From Contemporary Poems to Grave Robbing and
Home Wakes
© 2016 Favoritetrainers.com Books
ISBN: 978-0-9891696-4-6
This book is available on Amazon.com
Printed in the United States of America
Geramond 12 pt. interior
Cover photo courtesy Wikimedia Commons, free for public and
commercial use.

DEDICATION

This work is dedicated to the memory of many fine teachers at a certain small, rural school in southern West Virginia, including H. B. "Tommy" "Coach" Thomas, Rupert L. Blankenship, Ida Belle Pendleton, Ron Reed, Jack Richmond, Joy Bowman, and many others. They knew that the kids from coal mining and farm families deserved just as much, in everything.

Collection © 2016 Danny R. Kuhn

TABLE OF CONTENTS

Preface

Almost as lovely as your average tree.

There's a difference between singin' and sangin'.

But now, that doesn't necessarily mean nobody thinks it happened.

Real People.

Industrial deaths, grave robbing and home wake memories.

Contributor Biographies

Preface

In 2014, an old friend in West Virginia told me he wrote fantasy and mythology stories, but hadn't tried to get them published. I was between writing projects and suggested, on a whim, that we collect and edit an anthology of West Virginia-located mythology and fantasy. I put out the word on various writers' sites, and soon we had a collection of tales we really liked: *Mountain Mysts: Myths and Fantasies of the Appalachians* (Headline Books, 2015). We intended to self publish it, and only submitted it to a couple of traditional publishers to go through the motions. To our surprise, a great publisher liked it, West Virginia native actress Joyce DeWitt (*'Three's Company'*) endorsed it, and it was on its way.

Through that process, I had several inquiries from Appalachian writers who were not into fantasy, but enjoyed other types of writing. Do you know who might publish poetry? Even if its not of an Appalachian theme? Contemporary song lyrics? Traditional nursery rhyme form? How about memories of older relatives, stories about bygone burial practices in danger of being lost?

My second novel having been scheduled for a December 2016 release, I had some time before the manuscript for Number 3 was due. I decided to float the idea of a literary digest-style book of mixed poems, songs, and short prose, both non-genre fiction and Appalachian memory nonfiction. I wrote a few pieces myself, and remained open to a broad, eclectic collection based more on the styles that allowed the writers' voices to come through than my preset parameters.

For that reason, this final product is much different than the one I first envisioned. Two sections, *Memoir* and *The End*, are here solely because some of the contributors wanted to write those kinds of pieces, and I enjoyed the work so much that I couldn't turn it down. Some of the home wake memory writers are in their eighties, and have never before had anything published. They seemed genuinely happy that someone wanted to help them commit those memories, still clearly painful even after many decades, to the immortality of print.

In fact, though we have a few established authors represented in these pages, a *majority* of these writers have not previously been published. They represent a wide swath of modern Appalachia, from those who look back to walking the streets of Welch, West Virginia during its heyday as a coal boom town, to young artists writing their own songs to do gigs in Charleston and Lewisburg, and delivering pizza in once-thriving county seats.

Some of these writers are old friends, while others I have never met. But, a common thread runs through their writing. Do they bring civilization to the mountains, or is it the other way around?

Maybe *Not Taking A Fence* will help you answer that question. It did for me.

Danny R. Kuhn, M.A.   March 2016

Verses

Progress
Jonetta Bennett

Someday, I think I will
Go to the castle on the hill,
To tell m'Lord (for he must not know)
Of the plight these people have below.
His the land, his the flocks,
Our tenant plot barren rock,
With nine parts of ten going to him,
While our children starve, prospect grim.
But I trust he's benevolent, so go I must dare.
He would not let us suffer were he only aware.

Someday, I think I will,
Go to the big house on the hill,
To tell the owner (for he must not know)
Of the plight of the men mining his coal.
We have to buy food at the company store,
Though dollars instead of scrip would buy much more.
They cheat at the scales and fire union men,
This many widows and orphans must be a sin.
But I trust he's benevolent, so go I must dare.
He would not let us suffer were he only aware.

Someday, I think I will
Go to the mansion on the hill,
To tell the executive (for he must not know)
The minimum wage is much too low,
For us big box store clerks to pay our rent
And feed our kids. It was never meant
To keep us part time, without benefits,
Like health insurance or retirements.

But I trust he's benevolent, so go I must dare.
He would not let us suffer were he only aware.

Pride
Jonetta Bennett

There are times when country boys and girls
Leave the hollows and the hills
To make their way by going to sea,
Saying goodbye to family.
They find a life not like the farm,
Playing hide and seek in the barn.
A rope is a line, don't forget it.
Sleeping and bathing are not so private.
But they see England, or maybe Japan
And beautiful beaches of golden sand,
While mom and dad, not the modern type,
Want letters and calls 'cause they don't Skype.
But proud they are, and will always be
To say their kid is in the Navy.

Finding Them
Jonetta Bennett

"Cedar trees, honeysuckle vine, and rock lilies.
That's how you find them," she said.
"Cedars are holy, they built the Temple,
and their green won't fade in winter.
Honeysuckle covered the fences, now long gone,
To hide the smell on hottest days."
"And rock lilies?" I asked.
"The roots go deep, and suck you up.
The leaves are sharp, like swords, and they stand erect.
They say, 'Don't mess with me.' It happened, you know."

Michael's Reply to His Father's Violent Outburst upon Being Told He was Going to Marry James
Jonetta Bennett

"But Pop,
You always said
You didn't believe
In mixed couples!"

Charlie's Pub
Matthew Burns

I walked in to Charlie's pub
with that woman on my mind
sat down at the bar
and ordered tequila with lime.

"It seems like I've seen you before"
said the old man next to me,
"I recognize you by the hurt in your eyes
and the tears runnin' down your cheek."

I thought the old fool had lost his mind
and didn't give it a second thought
'til he asked this question
and put me on the spot.

"Son, I know you miss her
but is it really worth the pain?
You see, we've all been in your shoes
and played that losin' game."

His words caught my attention
but I didn't know what to say
I'd just come in to have a drink
Hopin' it would ease the pain.

He gave me a pat on the back and raised his glass
and said "Here's to livin' free!
It may take a while but you'll learn to live
like that man you used to be."

I raised my glass to his
and they resounded with a clink
Suddenly things didn't seem so bad
as I turned up my drink.

The lights seemed a little brighter
and the music was just grand
people were talking and laughing
and listening to the band.

I turned to thank the old sage
but there was no one in his seat
Then I spotted his picture on the wall,
it said "Charlie R.I.P nineteen ninety-three."

Florida
Matthew Burns

My sister moved to Florida
it's very far away
I fear she'll be eaten by an alligator
it could happen any day.

I hear they have big snakes down there
that grow larger by the hour
I hope if she ever encounters one
she doesn't get devoured.

I know there are many lizards there
and turtles by the score
they could easily carry her off
though it may take ten or more.

The mosquitoes are quite ravenous
I've heard many people say
I hope she buys some bug repellent
to keep such pests at bay.

I almost forgot to mention sharks
with teeth so sharp and jagged
at least they can't walk on land
otherwise they'd run us ragged.

But the number one danger of all
is the source of all our power
I hope she reapplies sunscreen
if out more than a couple hours.

Pizza Driver's Eyes
Matthew Burns

My life had reached its boiling point
and I didn't know what to do,
so I sought out something familiar
the only comfort I knew.

Now some would turn to religion
and some to alcohol,
some might look to heaven
while others just stagger and fall.

Me I deliver pizza
to the people of this town
You might think it's silly
but it's the most rewarding job around.

I don't make a lot of money
but that's not what I seek
I do it to see the smiling faces
almost every day of the week.

There is something to be said
about taking someone a pie
When steam rolls out of the hot bag
and you see a sparkle in their eye.

I provide the fuel
for people to live their life
to live laugh and love
through triumph and through strife.

I'm not going to say
that I'm some hero in disguise,
but the world looks a little different
through a pizza driver's eyes.

Bon Voyage
Matthew Burns

I bid her bon voyage this morning
before she left to cross the ocean
she's off to see a far off land
and I'm left filled with emotion.

Such beauty and grace I've seldom seen
as through this world I've wandered,
she's like the pot of gold at the rainbow's end
but this treasure cannot be plundered.

Tonight as I sit alone at home
and drink to her good fortune
the whiskey will flow, and perhaps tears too
but of the latter, only a small portion.

Someone Speaks
Evelina J. Butcher

I stand in a room alone,

Someone speaks,
But the words, I don't know.
While trying to explain their thought,
I merely nod yes.
All the while wondering in silent solitude,
If there was ever a person so misled as myself,
And so confused,
I stood in a room all alone,
Listening to someone speak.

A New Home
Evelina J. Butcher

If we should someday find ourselves in need of a new home,
If we should someday find that our world is beyond our means of
control,
With air pollution, holes in the ozone, loss of the rainforest and killing
off animals that used to freely roam,
Do you think we would find someone who would give us a new lease?
If we should find ourselves in need of a new home.

A Place to Sleep
Evelina J. Butcher

Now as I go to my bed to sleep,
A child cries in need of warmth and something to eat.
As I cover myself with a quilt of pink,
An old man lies covered only by newspaper in an alley.
As I rest my head on my pillow and drift off to sleep,
A man lies bleeding in the street.
As I dream in the comfort of my quiet room,
The runaways sell themselves,
For money and a place to sleep.

Attitude
W. M. D.

Tho' you may try your hardest,
'Til you think you've given everything,
There will always be a critic,
To tell you how it should have been.

Tho' you have fought many fights and won,
There will always be someone to say, "The battle has just begun."
When you think you have accomplished much,
There will be someone to say, "The surface is all you touched."

Tho' extra hours you have spent,
And not earned a penny more to pay the rent,
It's not all the fights you've won that is remembered,
But just the one you so long ago lost.

Be not discouraged, for everyone has a critic,
Take pride and know that you've done the best job you could,
In every man there is some good,
But it is only reflected from within through his attitude.

If We Knew
W. M. D.

If we could know what life had in store
In just the next minute or a little more
Would we live the way we do?
I'm not quiet sure, how about you?

Is there someone that you would tell
How much you loved them, or would you yell?
Would life be much different than it is right now?
If so, then tell me how.

Would the day seem a little brighter?
Would the mountain seem a little higher?

16

Would the river seem a little deeper?
Would that price tag seem a little cheaper?

Would that car really mean so much?
Or would you just want…to touch?
Would you let that last moment go by?
Or would you just sit down and cry?

A lot of things I suppose
Would be different if we knew what heaven knows.
But alas, time will always come and go
And we may never know what heaven knows.

So,
We shall journey on till tomorrow
And never let us think the sorrow
Of what life would be
If we really could know about tomorrow.

Coffee
W. M. D.

The machine grinds
The beans swirl…breaking up into millions of pieces
Suddenly the blade stops

The pieces thrust into the basket, quickly
The aroma begins to fill the air with the smell that can only be
described as
An essence of the earth brought forth on this glorious morning

The aromas is quickly sealed in a basket and covered with the hot
lifeblood of
The earth flowing across the broken pieces
Soon the aromas will escape and fill the room as a present from God
The black nectar fills the cup. Its dark, rich color is opaque
The steam rises and brings the godly aroma into the nostrils of the
once

Asleep body that is now brought to life for a new day. Not just a new day
But a new year that has been summoned by God
Once again time to be faithful and thankful.

Anti
W. M. D.

If we need to be Anti-something, then why don't we start with a few of these.....Anti-poverty
Anti-hatred
Anti-human trafficking
Anti-hunger
Anti-homelessness
Anti-injustice
Anti-abuse
Anti-children without fathers

Our Time On Earth
W. M. D.

Our time on Earth is short
We should live it to its fullest
One day of birth
One day of death
Life or death
Thank You for the in betweens
Maybe I complained too much
Maybe I didn't see the vision
Maybe I focused on the things that mattered little
Maybe sometimes I thought too big

Little, or big.
Thank You for the In betweens

For the good things
Life, love, marriage, children, friends, success,

For the not so good things
Pain, suffering, divorce, brokenness, failure,

Smile or tear
Thank You for the in betweens

Day...Night
Sunrise....sunset
Spring, summer, fall, winter
Heat...cold

Thank You for the in betweens
Mercy and Grace
Thank You for the in betweens

There Are People
W. M. D.

There are people that know everything
I don't

There are people that know why bad things happen
I don't

There are people that know why they are always on the right side of
thing
I don't

There are people that know that doing good things will unlock the keys
to heaven
I don't

Everyday I am challenge
My faith must be too small

I am on a journey
I don't know the path

People say you should be certain
My faith must be too small

Job was challenged
After all loss, Job stood fast
I wish I had the faith of Job

David stood at the valley facing Goliath
His faith kept him solid
I wish I had the faith of David

Paul was locked up
He rejoiced in being chained
I wish I had the faith of Paul

When people say that Christians are hypocrites
I am paralyzed

When people say you don't serve the widows and orphans
I am jolted

When people say the kingdom should be seen on Earth
I cringe

I am blessed but I am cursed

I want the best
I want to share
I want to love

My inner man is selfish
I try to throw him off.

Memories With My Dad
W. M. D.

I'm a lucky man
I have the best dad

Not perfect and not some TV sitcom dad
But a real dad who loves us no matter how old we all get
Maybe it's because we are older that it's the memories we cherish most.

The smell of a cigar
The smell of Old Spice aftershave
The thermos of coffee in his lunch bucket
Pepsi
Masonic ring
A set of Wilson golf clubs that he never got to use too much
The way the coal dust settled into his skin
The way he would sing in the car
The way he ruled we always knew where he stood
The way my mother's words, "Wait till your father gets home," could
strike utter fear into my brother and me.
The way four letter words could shake the house

The times he worked so hard
The times he worked second shift
The time he went to Florida because there was no other work
No one ever called him lazy

The time we drove to Virginia Beach for vacation and visited Uncle
Harold
The time we drove to South Carolina and went fishing with Uncle Jack
The time we went fishing on a boat and he lost his watch in the lake
The time we piled into the back of the station wagon with a grocery
bag full of popcorn to go see a movie at the drive-in

The time I took him to see "Close Encounters of the Third Kind"
The time he told a joke that was so funny, I spewed milk out my nose
The times we went to the Methodist church and I heard him sing
"Holy, Holy, Holy"
The time the Baptists ran off the preacher and the preacher came to
him for council
The time he went down to the school and threatened the teacher that if
anyone touched one of his children again, it would be the last time
No one called him a saint

The wisdom on the front porch that changed the direction of my life six weeks before I was headed to Marshall University to study pharmacy

The way cars and trucks impacted us
I remember the Ford Econoline and my Dad's wreck in the Bronco "half cab"

The time he folded down the windshield on the Bronco and we went for a ride through the hills and picked blackberries

The VW Beetle and how he taught me to drive the "stick" and in later years drove the Autocar coal truck over winding roads to Bristol, Virginia

The Buick LeSabre, Chrysler Cordoba and Datsun 510 wagon and sedan, and the Datsun 810 The F-150 and the GMC Sierra that I drove from Virginia to Buffalo, New York

The way he could use different means to build character and motivate I thought my brother and I were helping to build a house but instead we were building knowledge, strength and character

The way he taught me to use tools to work on the car and house and the wisdom of "Someday you might not have the money to pay someone else to do this for you so you better learn how to do it yourself." The way he would say, "Is that the best you can do?" and even if it were an "A" would say it with a smirk

Summer jobs and the way a number four shovel caused me to stay in school
The way he responded with "It's just a piece of metal." when I totaled the Chrysler Cordoba
The way he called me every week on the WATS line while I was at college just to check on me
The way he uncharacteristically responded when I told him I flunked my first Calculus test in college and wanted to drop out
He always wanted the best for us and not much for himself
We always knew we were going to college

When we asked him what he wanted for his birthday, Father's Day or Christmas, he would say, "Three smiling faces and a good word." Later it became "Five smiling faces and a good word."
I remember how proud he was when I graduated college

The number of people whose lives he touched
The way my friends could always come over to the house
The time Alan came to live with us
The time he drove through the night to get over to Logan County after the Buffalo Creek flood and brought back Tim and Rick to live with us
The time last year when Tom stopped me to tell me that my dad was the best boss he had ever had

So the four letter words I remember from my Dad today are
Work – do it well and give it your best
Love – it drives everything you do

Some called him "The Boss"
Some called him "Brother"
Some called him "Don"
Even though I have two sons of my own, I'm still proud to call him "Daddy"

Things I Never Knew
W. M. D.

I knew and was grateful for all that I could see
I never knew I should be grateful for being able to stand and pee

I knew that life was short
I never knew growing old could be so cold

I knew that every breath was a gift
I never knew how much energy it took to breath

I knew that hospitals were meant to save lives
I never knew how much life and dignity they stripped away

I knew that all of the technology was useful
I never knew how annoying the sound of pumps and alarms could be

I knew families were thrown into turmoil when a loved one was in
critical condition
I never knew how quickly waiting rooms could be transformed into a
cross between a slumber party and a homeless shelter

I knew 24 hour news existed
I never knew that it was really 1 hour of news repeated for 24 hrs

I knew I enjoyed food and eating slowly was better for you
I never knew how food could be de-constructed and how slow eating
could be

I knew I enjoyed eating with family
I never knew how it would feel actually feeding my dad

I knew that nurses worked hard, long hours in a noble profession
I never knew how demanding patients could be

I knew that nurses were smart people
I never knew that nurses who took time to give a patient a shave could
restore so much dignity

I knew recovery was slow
I never knew how many small important steps there were to recovery

I knew my dad was strong and independent
I never knew how dependent he could become

I knew going to a movie and fishing with my dad was fun
I never knew how much sitting by his side would mean

I knew that education was good
I never knew there would be so many things I wouldn't want to know

Mother
W. M. D.

Mother, for all the things you have done,
You were always the one

Standing behind me, holding me up
Standing beside me and pulling me out of a rut
Standing in front of me, helping me see
All the world that was ahead of me

You had other sons and daughters
But you made each one feel like they were the only one
And when they were gone
You quickly found
Many a kid to put on solid ground

You laughed
You cried
You felt every hurt and pain
You made each one see what they could gain

Never a child
Did you know
That you could not give an education
To make them grow

You were the defender of the weak
You sat on side of justice
All the things you did that seemed like nothing
Made the change in thousands of kids to make them something

We didn't always say
How we felt along the way
For the love you gave and the work you've done,
We want to say "We Love You and Thank You," including your
admiring son.

Thankful
W. M. D.

How can a person be thankful when they lose their mother? It is hard!

We never wanted to see my mother in a hospital...but we did.
We never wanted to see my mother in pain...but we did.
We never wanted to see my mother helpless...but we did.
We never wanted to see my mother die...but we did.

We are thankful that people have stopped up and allowed us to be in WV away from our jobs and other responsibilities during this period.

Our mother wanted to tell her 92-year-old mother that she was going to die soon. I was able to take her to see her mother. For that we are thankful.
Our mother wanted to update her will to leave what little money she had to the grandchildren's education. I was able to get her to the lawyer to do that. For that we are thankful.
Our mother never wanted to go to a nursing home. She did not. For that we are thankful.
Our mother never wanted to be in too much pain. With the help of medication it was minimized. For that we are thankful.
Our mother never wanted to suffer through chemo or Alzheimer's, or be a burden on others. She did not. For that we are thankful.
Our mother did not understand the tremendous positive impact she had on others until we read her the CaringBridge posts. For that we are thankful.
Our mother loved flowers. In her last days in hospice, we had a dozen yellow roses delivered like my dad had done. She saw them and commented how beautiful they were and how good they smelled. For that we are thankful.

For all the wonderful doctors nurses and technicians, we are thankful.
For hospice and the wonderful work they do, we are thankful.
For the ability for all of the children and most of the grandchildren and brothers and sisters to visit with our mother, we are thankful.
For the ability to spend time and talk with her and tell her that "I love you," we are thankful.

For having a mother whose faith and conviction never wavered, we are thankful.

For having a mother that knew how to forgive, we are thankful.

For having a mother that sacrificed her own needs for her family, we are thankful.

For having a mother that had a passion for education, we are thankful.

And we are thankful for humor.

What If
W. M. D.

What If...I had been kinder
What if...I didn't think I was right so often
What if...I said Thank You more
What if...I had not been so critical
What if...I had encouraged more
What if...I had given more
What if...I didn't see barriers where there were none
What if...I wasn't afraid what people would say
What if...other people are like me
What if...

What If...We had been kinder
What if...We didn't think we were right so often
What if...We said Thank You more
What if...We had not been so critical
What if...We had encouraged more
What if...We had given more
What if...We didn't see barriers where there were none
What if...We weren't afraid what people would say

The Sojourner
W. M. D.

The West Virginia Hills welcome the sojourner
The lush green of spring envelops him

He has been gone too long
His life has become too busy

The car rounds the corner and crosses the yellow lines
The hairpin curves are straightened by a mountaineer driver

Out of the corner of his eye he catches a glimpse of a herd of deer
standing in the field
He recalls how the concrete jungle is void of wildlife

His gut hurts for a day gone by
A day when he was at peace

His mind and soul rush back to a time of peace and playfulness
The hills call out "Welcome Home"
And he is....Home

Where I Find Myself
W. M. D.

I once knew where this life led
But that was before
Before they were dead

I once knew how to dream
But that was before
Before when my thoughts were light and clean

I once knew what to do
But that was before
Before life was askew

There was a day
Or was it a week?
A week that seemed so ever bleak

There was a week
Or was it a month?
A month that was filled with tasks that seemed to never pass

There was a month
Or was it a year?
That changed so much to doubt and fear

The mountains provided comfort
A place removed and protected
A home where none are rejected

Come as you are
The hills open wide
Your hopes and dreams are safe inside

The chasm between the hills seems so great
But the grandeur and beauty
Of the color of fall, you cannot wait

A wander down to the pond
Provides a peaceful rest
Where the mind and body become their best

Between heaven and earth, a life suspended
Between faith and doubt, a life extended
This is the place where I find myself

The Ormolu Clock
Justin Di Cristofaro

My mind is composed of malignant gears,
like that of a gilded Death Clock,
generating words like hours,

striking my right hand to speak for me-
when my mouth cannot.

Sleeping With Ghosts
Justin Di Cristofaro

We are always told not to live in the past,
but in my life the past is the only thing that is certain.
The present becomes past, and the future, exhausting- and blurry.
I don't sleep to dream, rather, I sleep to remember.
Memories replay themselves on an antique projector,
as if they are telling me a bedtime story.

One Night In Westminster
Justin Di Cristofaro

I could tune out the sound of the unruly streets,
by watching you write over your shoulder.
I was *The Virgin Suicides* and you, *The Bell Jar.*
Occasionally you would write a line of hope that reminded me of
home,
and even sometimes write a line of love that reminded me of my
parents.
Still yet, there we were, Jayne Eyre and Voltaire in your Westminster
apartment.

Aquarian
Justin Di Cristofaro

If one day you should ever ask where I've gone,
don't lay ears to the ground but to the sea.
Deep in water I am suspended,
unbound by the need to breathe.
I am home.
I am free.

77 South
Justin Di Cristofaro

White noise on the radio,
takes me back years ago.
There are cracks in this mirror...I know.
Strangers keep passing me.
The headlights are blinding me,
and there is pain on both sides of the road.
I can lose control of it.
I can slam the brakes on it,
but there is still twenty miles to go...

Imaginary Boys
Justin Di Cristofaro

Imaginary Boys
I heard once, that when a bitter fruit grew from the Tree of Life, it fell
and rot into the ground,
and the seeds gave rise to this place.
The endless forests are gray from a variety of lifeless trees,
and the sky is thick with smoke.
It's home.
I could imagine hundreds of places like this one.
All places that God had forgotten about.
A place like this breeds a certain type of boy.
Boys like us.
At birth, we brought a piece of death with us,
a permanent connection to this world,
and another full of suffering.
A rope ties us between heartbreak and the earth.
Imaginary boys,
each created by the other to prevent either from going completely mad
in a world like this one,
we've been damned here for our unhappiness.
When the trees swallow the skyline, we tell stories,
stories from our dreams,
to pass the time.

This gives way to many dangers.
When one spends so much time in dreams,
the line between dreams and our lives
starts to fray.

There Once Was a Man
Renee Haddix

There once was a man I knew
Passing by each day, a kiss he blew
Turning my cheeks into a bright red blush
Glancing his way, my head would rush

Dark brown hair and grass green eyes
Honey-toned voice that liked to lie
Saying he'd walk thirty-five thousand miles
Just so he could see my pretty smile.

Seven years, my senior, fourteen and twenty-one,
My Papa said to him, "Now, son!
Get on down the road lest you meet my gun!"
With a quiver in my chin, I thought he'd run!

Head held low and moving slow
Mise' well be walking to death row
Defeat and sadness inside him flowed
Used his shirtsleeve to wipe his nose.

My papa said, "He's simply no good.
I'd let you have him if I could!"
Anger flooded me where I stood,
Stomping my feet upon the wood.

"Papa!" booming loud I bellowed
"That's the man I love! My fella!
You sent him away looking down a gun barrel
I'm going to get him, my heart's in peril!"

So off the wooden porch I jumped
Hair flying back, I felt so pumped
A quick glace back, my papa looked stumped
I had to find my one true love.

Dust clouds rose beneath my feet
Around the bend I knew we'd meet!
He turned in time, surprised to see
A breathless, crazy, hopelessly in love, me!

Taking a roll onto the ground
Our heartbeats pounding, the only sound
His hands, my hands, everywhere,
So hot and bothered, not a care.

Unheard to my rushing ears, footsteps fell
Leaves crushing beneath big feet, I heard a gasp.
Papa was there to complete his task,
His meaty finger about to pull the trigger.

"Move your hands one more inch, I dare ya!"
Papa snarled, enough to scare ya.
My fella froze and then arose
Face turned white, trembling, a sight,
Looking down the inside of the cold hard barrel.

Holding my hand, he took a stand.

"Mister, don't shoot me! I didn't commit a crime!
Love is like a nonsense rhyme,
Sometimes it makes a perfect fit
Like an ole' hound dog that a flea just bit,

Getting down into your skin
It's an itch that don't stop itchin'
Time and time again!
Sir, I know that she's your special kin
But I love this girl and will til the end!"

Papa held tight to his gun that night

Fingers about to squeeze.
Looking over at his baby girl
He could see her eyes shine bright.
That's what made papa freeze.

He shook his head with remembrance
Of what love felt like in his day.
Pictures of lovers stealing each other away.
Lowering his gun, he said he was done.

"You can love her, son,
But make no mistake, young man,
My heart is hers, and if it breaks
It's your heart that I'll take.
That's a promise that I make!"

So the years went on and on
And I'm still loving my handsome fella.
A life we built, a family we have
While Papa's gun stayed firmly on the mantle.

Almost Heaven
Renee Haddix

Falling from the stars into the lap of heaven
Tucked between majestic mountains so grand
Glorious land where green grass grows
Constant current of the river flows
Unmovable rocks remain the same
Solitary leaves blowing
In the warm September rain.

Fairy tales and lullabies
Renee Haddix

Fairy tales right before bed
to my little ones were read,

singing lullabies about our life
saying prayers for no strife,
their sweet dreams lay just ahead.
Heads on pillows, all comfy to sleep,
Eyes slowly lowering, yawning deep.
Go to sleep, my little ones I say
So you can wake up to a brand new day.
Shut your eyes now and count some sheep.

Carefully down the hall I sneak
With my heart so full, I barely speak.
Crawling in bed, to cuddle with my love,
I'm thanking the Good Lord high above.
I should shout if form the mountain peak.

So blessed am I, my thanks I give.
So happy, so full, for the life I live,
Not boasting, nor gloating, just happy to be
Settled with my little family
To happily live, laugh, and love.

Color in My World
Renee Haddix

Before you were born into what was once my bleak world
The only colors in sight were merely black and white
But then the sun arrived, bundled you up in a colorful swirl,
Eyes as dark as chocolate, you made my heart whirl.

I loved you
Before I knew you.
I loved you
Before you breathed your first breath.
I loved you
Before I held you.

You were kissed by the heavens, while falling from the stars,
Your hair is spun gold, you fell into my arms,

To hold and to dream, to hope and believe,
You are a beautiful blessing that I received,
Borrowed from the stars, a gift was given to me
To raise, to love, to teach, to cherish,
To enjoy her and all her rarest moments,
To hold, to let go, to watch her grow.

I loved you yesterday, today, and tomorrow,
Until time runs out and there's no sorrow,
Until the moon can no longer borrow
The sun's rays to shine on our tomorrow.
That's how long that I'll love you.

I loved you
Before I knew you.
I loved you
Before you breathed your first breath.
I loved you
Before I held you.
I'll love you til my dying breath.

Smart Kid in Appalachia
Sabrina Jones

The struggle is real for the smart kid in Appalachia.
Born to the rigid mountains of blue-black collar coal mine country
I cut my teeth within the confines of un-culture
Developing a fractured, sheltered identity
Spawned from the narrow-minded, the bigot...
Ahem.
The honest, hard-working, simple, and proud.
The last generation of a dying tribe trying to firmly ground its roots.
And limbs. And fruits.

My parents say I read too much.
Git ya nose outta that book if you wanna learn sumpin.
But aren't books educational?
Gittin' too big for your breeches, that's what.

I get scolded for blowing Christmas money on classics.
Be like your sister. Tomagotchi and Z. Cavaricci.
And do her homework. We cain't do no fractions.
Thank God and Satan for the library.
I hoard and hide stories to devour post-bedtime.

Once high school hits, I am too school for cool.
Instead of having curves, I break curves.
Earning evil glares from classmates who don't study,
I learn the southern way -- sit down, shut up, play dumb
Miss a question or two, feed the dog my homework, never raise my hand
Scale it back.
Too smart for my own good.
I must avoid being what Plath was – "too dangerously brainy."
So I bury my brain in pop culture, fads, and coal dust.

Still, I can't shake the smarts disease.
I don't marry a coal miner and have a litter of young 'uns after high school (or before).
With the wind to my face, I find my people, find my place.
I go off to "college" (snide snickers – too big for her breeches)
And return with degrees to the preacher calling me Dr. Fahrenheit.
I return -- to give books as gifts to the limbs and fruits.
An educator and a life-long learner
Who doesn't mind small britches and being too school for cool
If it makes the struggle less real for the smart kid in Appalachia.

Up on the Knob
Marion Kee

My eight-year self is watching
you as you are huddled out here smoking
grapevine at eleven,
and your choking
mouth is green around the gills but you
don't want to show it
and I'm giggling even though I know

that right now you don't think it's funny--
but you will.

My ten-year self is watching when
you come up after dark,
to light a cigarette, the one you took
from Aunt Jean's purse
you look around behind you first,
you tell yourself and me she'll never see
the missing but
she does, of course.

I am laughing 'cause you're sneaking so,
laying low just like the time
your Daddy caught you stealing melons,
hided you so good you
couldn't sit.

My sweet sixteen is watching while you're
lighting up a joint, against the war you claim,
the smoke is blowing sideways in the wind--
you could be standing in a draft. I ask,
but you won't say,
and I decide it's better to pretend
I'm sure you're not.

My twenty-something watches as you're
out here with a bottle and some
friends to toast the absent
where your Baptist Mom can't even
spot your grown-up lighter's glow.

We are laughing cause we're sneaking so,
laying low just like the time
we tried to get away with
drinking coffee at a tender age.

And you and me at half a century or so have shed
the old folks in some ways we never
dreamed of then.

Before the graveside service out here climbing up again
in need of cellular refreshment
can you even find one bar,
and which direction?
I am watching as you're pushing buttons--
tell me
show me
face me
can we laugh and
can the old folks hear you now?

4-5-5-4
Danny Kuhn

The scent of life
in lengthening days
is justly welcomed,
though mud-covered.

Finished the work,
laid back in the sun,
grass tickling the skin.
Youth remembered.

Once, bright smells reigned
down in the hollow.
But now tannic, dank,
smell of decay.

Sycamore leaves
pushed along by wind,
make the sound of rain,
winter brittle.

Just Above the Bluestone Dam

Eunice Lewis

Ah yes, it's covered over now,
With water cold and deep
But our memories are strong and warm,
As o'er the years they creep
To the old log house with the fireplace,
And the river road of sand
Where we walked along, fifty years ago,
Just above the Bluestone Dam.

Our feet were bare, but our hearts were gay,
As we played on a grapevine swing
While our brothers' fiddle and banjo rang,
We would dance and laugh and sing
And scoff at tales of the haunted bridge,
Where an invisible horseman ran.
Our childhood was a happy one,
Just above the Bluestone Dam.

The springhouse and the old Lick Spring,
I can taste that water yet.
From the stands of bees under locust trees,
We had honey one can't forget.
The butter and milk from our brindle cow,
Went well with the grand smoked ham.
We ate our fill of country grub,
Just above the Bluestone Dam.

We fished and swam, climbed and ran,
Where the water birches swayed.
While Mom washed clothes with lye soap,
We children laughed and played.
We carried water in wooden pails,
Oh life there was so grand.
Never can I forget those hours,
Just above the Bluestone Dam.

Our education, quite limited,
We got at a one-room school.
Where we sat on benches carved from logs,
To learn the "Golden Rule."
In gingham dresses and plaited hair,
We ate lunch of bread and jam.
Carried from home in a tin lunch box,
Just above the Bluestone Dam.

The old log church called Bluestone View,
At the top of John Pence Hill.
Folks for miles around in wagons came,
Seems I can see them still.
There was Blind Joe, Old Tom Pack,
Aunt Suzy and "Groundhog" Sam.
They worshipped every Sunday there,
Just above the Bluestone Dam.

There's the Sunnyfield Cemetery,
Mom is resting there.
She gave her old sunbonnet up,
For a crown of gold to wear.
She had worked so hard to rear us right,
Then she joined the angels band
And left her earthly home behind,
Just above the Bluestone Dam.

When life's golden sun shall set for me,
I shall meet those gone before
And we will be so happy,
When we greet loved ones once more.
I will be so glad to see them,
And shake their friendly hand.
We shall reminisce of childhood days,
Just above the Bluestone Dam.

Ed. note: This poem, by the late Eunice Lewis, was previously published in the program for the world's largest family reunion, that of the Lilly family, held annually in Flat Top, West Virginia. The first reunion was held in 1929, and it grew to include grandstand shows by nationally known entertainers, carnival rides, baby-kissing politicians, and thousands of distant-relative attendees. Still held today, it is listed in the *Guinness Book of World Records* as the largest event of its kind.

"Home Of The Blue Demons"
Paul Lubaczewski

The righteous cheers
The laughing jeers
Team song
Long gone

The looming industry
The pageantry
The throngs
All gone

The trash they made
They left, it stayed
Like graves
It stayed

Those left behind
On hard times
They're stuck
No luck

I Hear Him Talking
Samantha Mann

I hear him talking. I don't know what he says.
I try to listen to other things, but he is so loud
I start to take offense, but my curiosity takes over.
I listen and realize he is talking about me.

I can see his black and white chest moving
With each breath he can speak volumes.

He is beautiful and comical, with his read head.
I wonder why he comes here to the hills.

The others aren't listening. They were busy like me.
The ones in the trees don't even care.
The gray ones wag their tails in quick jerks, telling their own stories.
The red ones are busy on the ground.

He tells me that he doesn't want me here and that I don't belong.
He sings it out of duty because it is his job, after all.
I finally get frustrated and argue back. "Don't pick on me, I do belong here!"
He doesn't listen. He just keeps complaining and we all try to ignore him.

I try to tell him, "I belong here."
I belong because my parents did and their parents before them.
They are here still. A part of earth.
Didn't you see the stones we raised to mark their place in the hills, the fence to mark the boundary?"

He becomes quiet and darts to another tree.
He looks at me as if he is pondering what was said.
Maybe he understood about ancestors.
Maybe he remembers his parents and they are also in this earth.

He starts again with renewed vigor, telling me to leave.
He doesn't understand markers and fences.
This mountain is his, but he doesn't say why.
He only says, "You don't belong here."

I glance at the raised stones. For a moment, I agree.
The stones are dark and shiny. They really don't belong here with the other stones.
The fence is annoying to the sapling trying to rise around it.
He offends me with his chatting, but I offended him first, I suppose.

I consider moving the stone and find that I can't breathe.
My vision blurs and my chest tightens.
Will I be okay if there is no stone?

It will look like every other hill in West Virginia, and there are a lot of them.

I can't listen to him anymore.
I yell at him and throw rocks, run and chase him through the trees.
I try to end his song, change it. It must change!
They all run away and hide from me. The song stops and only silence remains.

Snowcapped Mount
Sarah McHatton

Off in the distance
High above me
Is a white dome
Of Smoky

Shivering with cold
Amazed with wonder
At the snow capped
Rise over yonder

Winters in these hills
Are so unpredictable
But the beauty
Almost touchable
    I surrender, the majesty
    And the wonder

The Markers
Sarah McHatton

The road was quiet and abandoned
Hidden with glens and bends
Like a moment in time, candid
All of life transcends

44

Soft moss beneath my feet
Absorbing the sounds of walking
Allows me to be discreet
Like I am stalking

The stones jut from the earth
In large, weathered markers
Surrounded by a fence at north
Keeping the borders

Beneath the ancient oak and pine
I open the rigidity, old gate
And step into the divine
Carefully watching my gait

I stop, head back, and stare
Thinking of time gone by
Of loved ones saying a prayer
Sobbing while saying goodbye

Unsaid words slip the shadows
Hidden among the tombs
Sorrow blatant in the hollow
Like a sunflower blooms

Names etched into the stone
Concealed by moss and time
A life that should have shown
But now without a chime

In the quiet of the thicket
I can stand and see
A question of good or wicked
Here under the chestnut tree

Spring's Desire
Sarah McHatton

A desire takes over
The closer that spring gets
To feel the dirt
Slide through the fingers

To see the greenery grow
Tall and strong as buds burst
Releasing small flowers
Eager to reach for morning dew

Plants bend toward the sun
Revealing green leaves, curled
Furling and stretching out
Dancing in the wind

The want for warmth and growth
Overtakes every living thing
Wakening from slumber
By the warmth of the sun

Bees, hummingbirds, and butterflies
Are a sight for sore eyes
As the desire builds
For vibrant color's arrival

That desire will only strength
As time passes and life renews
For our life on earth
Is garnered by the sun
　　　　Warm in its radiance
　　　　Kind in its sustenance

Love without Condition

Sarah McHatton

Condition not your heart
For it leads to paths unknown
A place of struggle and strife
Where no rest is known
A life of languished love
Silenced in fear and anger
Only to hurt those around you
Give freely and savior
Condition not your heart
And love will flourish
Life will grow happy
And provide all to cherish
       Love without condition
       And love becomes all

Appalachian Song

Sarah McHatton

The road is broken and battered
By the onslaught of winter's icy grip
Years of wear and tear breaking tar
A path returning to the ancient past

As it once was when Cherokee
Walked the paths between the mountains
Searching for the hunted and prey
Creeping through the trees

Ivy creeps across the blacktop
With thin tendrils reaching for a grasp
To pull themselves along the ground
Gaining foothold among the cracks

Shadowed by hundred year old trees,
I am taken aback in peace and tranquility

It overcomes my injured soul
Seeking a moment's peace

Underneath the trees, a chill rises
Twirling between the branches
Shielded from the harsh summer sun
To create the perfect place

I stop the car, amid the oak and pine
Entranced by the nature around me
A creek, crystal clear and unpolluted
Babbles over the ancient bedrock

I know that it seeks any free space,
Carving a path of its own
Like the mighty bear, paw to the ground
Thrashing through the forest

The knowledge of its time and beginnings
Fresh in my mind, I step deeper
Into the cool surroundings and listen
I listen for the song

Ancient and bone numbing, a connection
To the ground beneath my feet
To the air filling my lungs, the sound in my ear
The space, so hidden and so unscathed

Something so easily severed
Amid the modern trappings
Yet, I can feel the currents
Rising from the ground and into me
As a child of Appalachia
Forever rooted in the song
Something so powerful and tangible
Like notes rose from a banjo

Standing with hands on hips, eyes closed
Face turned toward the morning sun
I feel the energy, the love, and the toil

Of all those gone before me

In this moment, memories come
A whisper of a song, a word unspoken
Answered deep within my breast
As if touching my soul
        Appalachia, so wild
        And a melody so deep

Autumn in the Smokies

Sarah McHatton

The sound of rustling echoes through the valley
Sharp and long as the wind blows
Across the road, leaves of many colors
Tumble across the black asphalt

The red and yellow leaves of the birch
Rattle against the bark in a dry scrape
As they break off and float in the wind
Exposing the stark whiteness

Orange and brilliant against the pale blue sky
The maple shakes and shimmies
With a silent dance choreographed
To display the color of beauty

A spectrum of yellow with almond shaped leaves
The hickory follows suit with dancing
Pecans, chestnuts, and apples fall to the ground
In a loud 'thunk' that breaks open the fragrance

The shift of life takes on a new meaning
Of silence and solemn-ness
As all seem to prepare
For the onslaught of bitter, wet winds

Scents of burning hickory, bitter and sweet
Curl into the air, dotting the mounts
A quiet installs, shivering with new energy
Settling in for autumn's bounty

This I Wonder
Raymond Neely

Rile the farmers, the workers,
they grit and their guts tighten?
Convince them to holler
and louden the ancient eroded hills
about their cause?
Or raise the dirt poor,
those coughing and sickened
dwelling amid the dilapidation of drug addiction
and economic failure
of dying coal towns
into the sterile new age movements
of therapy, medicine, and counseling
which treat a population?
A flag or cry or cause
for I have trod among them,
have watched and met eyes and spoke with
this local area of people,
and as a fair and honorable one,
as a misplaced messiah,
but on an even keel with them all?
I heard their stories,
their opinions,
seen them torn and ragged gripping
their prejudices,
infected with wrong tradition,
but stubborn and proud
in a more beautiful world than once was.
Or cause movements of poets,
of artists,
an Appalachian renaissance,

finding the sheer and unmistakable,
unsurpassed intelligence of its ones,
virtuosos,
and as often blessed with talent
as those of anywhere,
and design a living network
Of our finest?—This I wonder.

I Ask the Mountaineer
Raymond Neely

Why go and seek out the world in
far away places when you
can't even come to know the place
you are from?
when, now more than ever
the world comes to you?

Young artists from our region
always ask
should I stay or should I go?
undoubtedly because of
the inopportunity perceived
to be our local trait,
beyond that mountain pass
into all of the carrying on
of the world
and the extra opportunity
of more well to do societies.

Nay, I say.
remain with the sanctity of
nature's enlightenment,
you mountain people and poets.
Enough of the world is linked
into you and passing through you.
Stay your mantra of the mountains,
in love with the forest,

enchanted by landscape
so you create more as god
and your arts ascend
as members of the forest toward heaven
and you benefit us all.

Beware
Raymond Neely

Tense, wiry,
hicks, hillbillies
spit in the dirt and spray
cuss words like spitting snakes,
burn eyes and lungs,
clench their tight small fists,
their twisting arms
and hit 'cha ya in the eye.
Then they'd be amused
grouped together behind
a row of pick-ups.
Scraggly, unkempt young'uns
tell you in a wide-eyed, serious,
as a matter of fact way
who the best banjo pickers are,
and where to find the best
moonshine,
spit and shoot pool in a beer joint.

Woodsmen, mountaineers,
keen and mean,
the serious slits of their eyes
sly snakes, killers,
but smarter than you,
cut your throat
attack you diagonally
like the single tooth of a wolf
and dump you in a sink hole or hollow
and never again think of you.

You'd be a long dead and gone family secret.

Mean fire in the stove,
behind a grate,
and a burning gizzarded old man
sitting on a bucket with a jug,
holed up in a trailer
like an angry possum,
uses backhands
and gravelly hollered commands,
family or foe,
scratched from the thicket,
hickory woods,
hell bastards,
broken backs.

Bad cussin's men gave,
suicide back in the mountains,
some shot in the head.

Four Verses
Janet Ransom

1. Lord, please forgive me
For my sins
I'd like to promise
I won't do them again.
But we both know,
You and I
I'm only human, Lord
But yes, I'll try.
Amen

2. Thank you Lord,
For being infinitely kind
For providing shelter

To our hearts and minds
In a tragedy
For letting us peek
At what's in store
But saving the brunt
When we can handle more
With your love.
Amen

3. I don't like ladders
I don't like them at all.
I don't think it's the ladders
But actually the fall.....

4. I try to help
I really do
There's not much
That I can do
I empathize
With your pain
But I can't feel it
Just the same
You are loved
Is all I can say
It's never enough
At the end of the day
But it's a start....

For the Spirit
Janet Ransom

The older we get
The harder to hear
The harder to see
Another one's fear.
The older we get
The less we see "lonely"

And when that love passes,
We think "if only."
Reach out to our elders
And the shut-ins we love
We need to connect
Before they go above.

Have you got a loved one,
Maybe living out of town?
Maybe age is creeping up
And maybe joy is falling down.
Don't wait another minute
Please don't waste another day
Just pick up a phone and call them
If only to say hey..
An open door, opens hearts.

When the daylight came,
And caught me asleep..
Of old friends and family,
I did dream.
When the daylight came,
And the dreams dissipated...
My heart broke again
And I did weep.

On my poorest day
I am richer than most
For in my heart
Lives the Holy Ghost.
Amen

Whippoorwill
Linda Lester Tabor

The sun goes down behind the hill
The twilight calls to the Whippoorwill
Through the fading light, I hear

The treasured tune, I hold so dear

Whippoorwill, oh, whippoorwill, singing in the night so still
oh your song it is so sweet
It makes its way to Heaven's feet, and, the angels hear that song
they all want to sing along

They make their way, to this fair earth, to the place of my mountain
birth
As they gather round my bed, that lullaby is gently led,
to all things gathered, near, and far
to rock to sleep, under moon and star

Midst my dreams, though I may roam,
I always come back to my mountain home
Back to the call of the whippoorwill
as shadows dance, on the windowsill
when setting sun, meets eventide
It is then, you're by my side

Whippoorwill, oh whippoorwill singing in the night so still
With your song, the memories pour, into my heart, until once more,
Your lullaby carries me to sleep, while the angels, around me keep
Outside my cabin, just down the hill, I hear your song, my sweet
whippoorwill.

Apple Tree
Linda Lester Tabor

Placing the wood on the glowing coals, I am amazed at how, with even
a few embers, if given just the right amount of air and space, a raging
fire can emerge from those radiant cinders.

It occurs to me, the wood, that now hisses and cracks as the flame
grows, was the apple tree from my backyard.

As a young girl of eight or nine, I climbed that tree, then, realizing I
was in over my head, called for my dad to come help me down. But,

56

soon enough, with much practice, I navigated those limbs and branches almost to the top. It was there, I learned to dream.

Sitting amidst the pink and white blossoms, I envisioned places and times far beyond my reach at that moment.

Through the turning of the years, that old apple tree became my sanctuary. Lying across her long, bulky limbs, my mind would visualize a certain someone that had captured my attention and my affection.

How sweet was the innocence of the young love. Seeing him in the hallways at school filled me with anticipation, and, such strong emotion, I could hardly bear witness to it. When he broke my fragile heart, I retreated to the safe haven of that flowering apple and wept for love and it's loss. And, I discovered, life moves on, and so too, must we.

In my memories I hear the carefree laughter of teenage girls. Under the shady branches, we lay there on that worn cotton blanket, looking skyward and wondering, if, we too, would ever journey to distant places, like the people we saw through the leaves of my apple tree, flying in airplanes, chasing the clouds.

Now, sitting in the quiet calm, only a Sunday morning can tender, I place another stick or two of wood on the fire and it comes to me that what started out as a seedling, had fully lived and fulfilled it's purpose.

It welcomed me as a child with the enticing fragrance of spring blooms, securing the promise that summer was just around the corner.

Those soft petals had played catch with my tears, when I grieved for what had escaped me, and for the emptiness of my heart.

Her leaves and boughs, held, loyally, all my secrets, my hopes, my fears.

Her life was not ended the day she no longer stood tall and green, but simply, found a new way to be.

She now gives me warmth, in the same way she sheltered me from sun and rain.

When the fire is gone and only ashes remain, they will be scattered on the brown earth, where, in the early days of spring, my garden will awaken, and come to life.

She will be a part of every flower and herb that calls my garden home. Her soul will forever be united with the spot her roots first felt the cool dampness of the ground.

She had the finest qualities of any friend I have ever known. Keeper of secrets, a listening ear, a gentle spirit.

She let me discover, while sitting on her outstretched limbs, that life is series of joys, sorrow, learning, and teaching.

She had stood in hushed grace, watching me grow, urging me, with each passing year, to climb higher, but reminding me that the most sturdy branches were those somewhere close to center.

If I climb too high, by the time I make my way down, my legs tire, and they feel shaky as they search for the solidness of the ground.

The top is a grand place to be, but only if I am aware of the balance it requires, and remain alert to the distance that separates me from the bottom.

Not climbing high enough, not risking going past the lower set of branches, is safe, and, more secure.

But, I have to wonder, what wondrous view I may be missing out on by not letting go of worry, and, making myself ascend just a few branches higher....

But the center, for most of us, is a near perfect setting. High enough to feel the wind dance all around, swaying the branches from side to side, but, not so that we have to tighten our grips beyond what is comfortable. The surest way to lose our grasp is holding on too tightly. From the center, looking upward, with clarity beside us, we can be given a glimpse of what awaits.

Below us, we can see, with keen accuracy, where we've been, what we've done, and the road that led us there.

And she thought, she was only a backyard tree.... Her legacy, was teaching me, we are always more than what we think.

Rivertown
Tony Wegmann

We got a dirty river trying to get clean
best looking women you've ever seen
she wears a gold dome like a crown
here in my river town
got mounds where the Indians lived
they tower just like pyramids
I hope they're never torn down
there part of our river town
we walk on streets named for the ones
that built this town up for our daughters and sons
be thankful that they were once around
to build our river town
all the boats pass through the locks
and the merchants keep up their shops
we can all step back and be proud
living in our river town
don't matter which side your from
you're one of the founding father's sons
no one is a face in the crowd
we sing out in our river town.

Ten Nursery Rhymes
Simie Wilkins

Johnny, Johnny Hickory Split,
With a pack
on his back,
"Bring out your chairs, two bits a seat!
Plus a little dinner to eat,
For Johnny, Johnny Hickory Split!"

Coal bucket, coal bucket,
Ready for a rest.
"Hang me on the wall. I've done my best!"
"But I'll use you to put chicken feed in,
and carry potatoes to the bin,
Coal bucket, coal bucket!

Mr. Crawdad, Mr. Crawdad,
You lucky little man.
Just for fun, I'll turn my hand
To build you a pond, quick as a wink,
As long as you let the cow come to drink,
Mr. Crawdad, Mr. Crawdad.

Old Paw Paw, my Paw Paw,
You got dribble on your chin,
Cause you need to spit again.
I suspicion what Maw Maw will do
When she finds that 'backer you chew,
Old Paw Paw, my Paw Paw.

Go wind it up, wind it up,
That's a horrible sound,
Just like it's dying, going around.
But to buy us a 'lectric one, Daddy's too poor,
Can't even bend over, back's too sore.
So wind it up, wind it up.

David, David, our neighbor David
Thinks he's better than us
Because he don't chew and he don't cuss.
He stays in church 'bout half his time
But if you're starving, you won't get a dime,
From David, David, our neighbor David.

There's a crack, big ol' crack
In the windowpane.
Let's in the snow, lets in the rain.
We take turns on that side, me and brother Ned
'cause we'll get blamed for wetting the bed,

But it's the crack, big ol' crack.

Left over biscuit, just one biscuit,
I don't care if it's gone hard.
I'll soak it in milk and break it apart.
No time to talk, it would be the worst
If my brother got to it first,
That biscuit, left over biscuit.

My little kitty, what a pity,
Tried to hop a train to Morgantown,
Came up short, went down and down,
Hanging on with her little fingernails
'Til the Elk River bridge, where she fell,
My little kitty, what a pity.

Salmon, jolly salmon,
Fried up in a cake
That took my mama an hour to make.
Or maybe just a minute, I don't know.
Get down in my belly. It's time to go!
Salmon, jolly salmon.

Ed. note: Nursery rhymes are an old literary form, but few very early pieces survive because they were not considered all that important at the time. They seem to have had their origin in lullabies, with an ancient Roman nurse's song, "Lalla, Lalla, Lalla, aut dormi, aut lacta" perhaps being the oldest surviving example. It's meaning will still resonate with new mothers today, being translated as "La La La, either sleep or nurse!" By the mid-eighteenth century, many of our nursery rhymes had been printed, and there is conjecture that some, such as *Humpty Dumpty* and *Hey Diddle Diddle* had barely-hidden contemporary political meaning. Characterized by repeating, rhyming lines about everyday items or activities but often with absurd twists, they are easy for children to remember and chant. These modern, Appalachian-based examples fit the pattern, from the peddler repairing hickory split chair bottoms to the non-melodious tones of an old-fashioned Victrola that needs a boost.

Hunky Town
Joseph Wroz

Daddy said I couldn't go
Over to Hunky Town.
"Them people give you the evil eye,
then you get run over, or drown."

"But don't they work just like you,
every day down in the mine?
Ya'll ain't separated digging the coal,
And that seems to work just fine."

"That's different, girl, when you're underground,
All men's lives are the same.
A slate fall or explosion
Respects neither color, nor your name."

"Then why are we separate up here above?
Why not the same church or school?
They have polka dances and homemade wine.
Your talk being funny don't make you a fool."

"They pray to statues and eat wild mushrooms,
you just don't know 'em yet.
So you ain't going over to Hunky Town.
No more talk, my mind is set!"

A man of his word, he said no more,
But that night came a full moon,
Yes, I went wandering to visit my Joe,
And we best get married real soon.

Ed. note: The coal camps were commonly separated into three distinct communities: White, Black, and Immigrant. Regardless of actual origin, eastern Europeans were often referred to as "Hunkies," a rude term for Hungarians. This poem, which the author suspects mirrors his own family history, illustrates the permeability of social boundaries when love beckoned.

Rush Run

Joseph Wroz

Fishing trip
Just for fun,
Walked the track
With a pack
To old Rush Run.

Camp near the old tipple
In the ghost town.
A roaring fire,
"Put on that old tire!"
Pass the bottle and lay on down.

There's bound to be a graveyard.
Tree frogs begin to peep.
A screech owl. What was that?
Are there still any wildcats?
Wish I could just go to sleep.

I have never seen such a wash of stars.
This was once a thriving town
Was that a child's laugh I heard?
No, just the twitter of a night bird.
Now all the buildings tumbled down.

Do they still roam this place?
These families of times gone by?
Men who mined the coal
That burned as the young nation's soul,
Smiling down as I lie?

Daily
Joseph Wroz

Out the back door
The air stings my face,
Its sharpness making the acrid smell of smoke
Even more keen.

Stay in the path through the snow.
The bottom is icy now,
Compressed by many footsteps
Completing this mission.

The shovel handle is cold
Even through my gloves,
And the top layer frozen,
Requiring effort.

It isn't very good this year,
A lot of bone and slack.
But, it was twenty dollars a ton,
Delivered.

Carry both buckets in.
Don't drag the bottom on the snow!
Stomp it off my unbuckled galoshes.
Bringing in coal.

Payoff
Joseph Wroz

Pop bottle cap
Lead head nail,
Turn up the discriminator,
the handle from a pail.

Broken hatchet head,
Right in a hill of ants.

I wonder whose property this is?
One crawled up the leg of my pants.

Ah! A wheat back penny!
Really corroded, though.
Cut my finger on a sardine can,
Swung the mattock and hit my toe.

Why do I still do this?
I get a small blip.
It's starting to drizzle,
But, look! A piece of New River scrip!

Monochrome
Joseph Wroz

Black and white,
Slate dump and snow,
Labrador and thistle down,
As a matter of fact, the whole town,
Us over here
And them over there.
Why, I don't know,
But we're like that slate dump and snow.

Welch
Joseph Wroz

Pocahontas or Temple?
One's got Van Johnson!
Traffic backed up to Coney Island.
No space on the street,
Take the muddy lot and use your feet.
See you at the Cut Rate.
Hotel Carter, didn't go in.
Everybody's Lunch
Or maybe The Grill.

Blakely Field? What's going on?
New shipment, ladies gloves.
There's a Plymouth double parked.
Mr. Coleman yells a curse.
It's Saturday. We ain't in church!
Western Auto,
To test a tube.
Next door, big case of penny candy,
Smell of popcorn, roasted nuts.
Crowd changes, comes dusk.
I'll be old enough to stay
Someday,
'cause I know it will never change.

Songs

Country Song
Danny Kuhn

Chorus:
I'm a red tag special, in the grocery store of life.
When you picked me up and priced me, I knew you were so right.
But then you put me down again, and walked out with some fruit,
For a red tag special, you didn't give a hoot.

Now, not so very long ago, fresh is what they'd say.
As the housewives came along, shopping my way.
Now you don't even pinch or squeeze, and it makes me weep.
There's no need to think I'm stale, just because I'm cheap!

(Chorus)

Being a little overripe don't mean I'm not nutritious.
A bit of soft spot here and there can be mellow and delicious!
So take me home and peel me, for the time of your life.
But we have to use a different line, 'cause this checker is my wife!

(Chorus)

Come Back to Me
Tony Wegmann

I built a little cabin,
way back in the woods,
Made a promise to a little girl,
cause she was treating me good,
but she got restless,

traveling on her mind,
Pretty soon she was gone,
she left me far behind.....left me far behind
oh she likes the big city,
likes the neon lights,
the place without pity,
and she is staying out all night,
soon there will be trouble,
her sidewalk will crack,
she'll find the first bus,
and come right back.

COME BACK TO ME, COME BACK TO ME

I'm plowing my fields,
I'm chopping wood,
I don't have much money,
But the weather's good,
yes it's so quiet,
I keep looking to find,
my long lost love,
she left me far behind

COME BACK TO ME, COME BACK TO ME, COME BACK TO
ME, COME BACK COMEBACK TO ME

Why are you running around,
I need to hear your sound,
Where can you be found,
oh she likes the big city,
likes the neon lights,
the place without pity,
and she is staying out all night,
soon there will be trouble,
her sidewalk will crack,
she'll find the first bus,
and come right back.

St. Albert Hotel

Tony Wegmann

I run the Greenwich up and down your great waters.

I bring good news and bad to your sons and your daughters.

Make room at the levee when I ring my Bell.

I got a room at The St. Albert Hotel
and the rooms have linens and steam heat with style.
A welcome sight after traveling this river for many a mile.
make room at the levee when I ring my bell
I got a room at St. Albert's hotel.
We haul coal, we haul liquor, we haul salt from the works.
we haul traveling ladies, yes sir they're always a perk.
Tonight she has me under her spell
I need a room at St. Albert Hotel
When the water is high I'll be around
When the waters to low I may run a ground.
And in summertime I'll escape that river smell.
With a room at the St. Albert Hotel.
Kanawha Street is busy year round.
People come to trade goods from miles around.
the sight and the sounds are the best in the land
And at St. Albert Hotel you can hear a band.

I run the Greenwich up and down your great waters.

I bring good news and bad to your sons and your daughters.
Make room at the levee when I ring my Bell.
Save a room for me at The St. Albert Hotel
Save a room for me at The St. Albert Hotel

Mountain State of Mind

Tony Wegmann

Southern peaks hang so close
the Monongahela flowing slow
our hills and waters will live for all time
got a Mountain State of Mind.
feel the self-sufficient pride,
a wild spirit, we won't be denied.
everywhere are people you can't replace.
everyone here shares that love embrace.
We work hard to keep our family
giving thanks just comes naturally
we've all been blessed with this rich earth
a gift us Mountaineers receive at birth
God blessed us with these West Virginia Hills
People with generosity and back country skills.
best folks on earth you'll ever find,
l have in a Mountain State of Mind.

Fiction

Ginseng
W. M. D.

Logan County 1930

Life was hard but there were no complaints. Bertha stood strong. Although her husband had passed away she still had a family that needed her to put food on the table and heat the house. Cooking and cleaning were non-stop in the small coal town. The general store provided the anchor for the town. Although the sign displayed her husband's name, she was the steady force that kept it going. She sold everything that people needed; canned goods, shoes, material by the yard, nails, hammers, shovels, picks, and rock candy. About the only thing she didn't sell was moonshine. It wasn't that there wasn't a ready supply and a larger demand, her church upbringing and having the kids around just wouldn't permit it.

But the mountains provided something more: ginseng. Ginseng had medicinal properties that were not explainable, nor proven. Modern day scientists would call it witchcraft and the placebo effect. But for mountain folk, it was a 'natural cure' that was used in teas, soups and medicines to cure sickness, increase vitality, relieve mental and physical fatigue and prolong life. Lore had it that old lady Moses had been using sang since she was 10 and that was one hundred and ten years ago.

Nary a day went by that a 'sanger' didn't come into the store with the prized root.

On this particular day, a rough mountain man named Jess wandered into the store. His clothes smelled of the mountains. It wasn't a stench but city folk wouldn't think much of it. His hands were cracked and his nails were long. "Whatcha got?" Bertha said, knowing full well that he

71

had a pouch of sang. Jess replied, "I've got a pound or two of sang today, Bertha. It was hard diggin' but I know I got at least that much." He dumped his well-worn pouch on the counter. "Sure enough Jess, you got at least 2 pounds there," she replied. "'Cept, most of it is dirt. Now go shake that dirt off outside and I'll weigh it."

As she loaded the scale with Jess's ginseng, it was clear there was only about a pound. Still that was a good piece of diggin'.

"Well Jess, I ain't got no cash in the drawer today. Do you want a store credit or are you needin' sumthin' today?"

Back in those days you didn't have to worry about selling it. Whatever you could buy, you could sell. When she first started buying it was about $3 a pound and she sold it for $5. Coal miners were making about $1500 per year and farm hands were only worth a couple of hundred so selling sang was a good business and more dependable than the mines.

Out of the corner of Jess's eye, he spotted something, "Where'd you git that?"

"Some fool from Massachusetts, I think his name was Hodges, crashed into my front porch last year in the middle of the night. I told him he was going to pay for the repair but he didn't have no money. So he left me his fancy musical instrument. Said it was made of fine metal so I guess I can melt it down and sell it if I have to."

"You know, I have a hankering for music, Bertha. Just give me a store credit."

A week or so passed and Jess was back in the store with even more sang. Over the next months, just like clockwork, he returned and each time he asked for a store credit. Bertha was happy to give a store credit because it meant the customer was coming back and these days, she needed customers. Since they had to move from the farm when her first husband Robert died, paying for food was a chore. She couldn't collect eggs, milk the cow or slaughter a pig like she had done on the farm. Still, the store provided for her family and for that she was grateful.

The train whistle blew loudly and it shook the holler twice per day. Cars weren't common in those parts and Pat Moore walked the tracks to get to where he needed. His limp was noticeable but he rarely complained. However, after an especially rough week, he returned home and asked Donnie to fetch him a rag and some warm water. He unbuckled the leather from his stump. Donnie's eyes couldn't believe the blisters that he saw on his step-dad's leg. The pain that Pat endured and the life draining energy that Bertha endured as she watched the store and cared for the kids was the sacrifice that she and Pat were willing to make.

Today was different. It wasn't clear. The cloudy mist covered the mountaintop. In the background you could hear the train whistle.

Bertha was tired. Pat been gone for over twenty-four hours.

Before she knew it, it had been forty-eight hours.

And then she lost track of time.

He had been gone for days, which turned in the weeks.

Then one day, Jess the sanger came into the store.

"Bertha, you won't believe what I just picked. I was a walkin' down by the tracks and I found this."

The sight was horrifying. Bertha clinched her teeth.

Jess tossed his bag onto the counter. As he did, a peg leg rolled onto the counter. It was Pat's.

"What are you willing to give me for this?" he asked, always looking to make a buck.

With all the courage inside her that she could muster, she said, "Whadya think it's worth?"

"I reckon two bucks."

"Fine," she said without a quibble she just wanted to get rid of Jess. She opened the cash register and pulled out two bucks and tossed it to him.

The ornate register that spoke of grander times now housed two lone copper coins. As the door slammed, she bent over the store counter and began to sob.

Pat was really gone. She was alone....again.

She grabbed a cloth and wrapped the peg leg like a package and stuck it under the hidden compartment under the display case where no one would find it.

The three youngest kids ran around, Donnie and the two girls.

All she could think about was 'how was she going to provide?'

Ginseng

Sure, the root had provided some dollars for her to make ends meet but could it do something more.

A trip to Lady Moses should prove fruitful but she dreaded the trip. Just like Moses' trip to the top of Mount Sinai, going to see Lady Moses was an emotional, spiritual and physical climb. Some folks thought she got her name because of the flowing robe she wore and the walking stick she used. There had been tales of her doing miracles. Kids often said that her hair and 'whiskers' made her look like a man. Most men thought she was crazy and her name was drawn from the fact she had been wandering the wilderness for over 40 years and probably knew the original Moses personally.

She'd sent the kids off to school that Tuesday morning before she headed up see Lady Moses. The world was about to change forever.

She gathered up her apron and pulled all the ginseng out of the display case and carefully weighed it...six pounds, three quarters. With her other hand she snatched the cloth wrapped package from under the display case. She hoped it would be enough to please Lady Moses.

74

She walked up the holler about 3 miles looking and searching for that wormy chestnut tree marking the entrance on the hillside for Lady Moses' place. It really wasn't a hillside. It was really a mountain climb that was only fit for a mountain goat. But knowing she had no other choice, she moved her rickety bones up the mountainside.

In 1930, sixty-five was an unusual age to still be living and doing the work that Bertha was doing. So climbing up the mountain like a goat was no easy feat. She slipped several times as her well-worn brogue shoes slid across the mud of the newly damp leaves. The smell of old musky earth filled her nostrils. It was a different smell than she remembered the last time she saw Lady Moses.

On her last trip to see Lady Moses, she recalled Lady Moses telling her she would be back.

On that trip, just after her first husband died, she was unwilling to up the ante. After all, the older boys were still at home helping with the farm. Although, she had found great resolve and had the strength to run the farm at that time, it was different now. She was still the strong willed woman but she felt she had lost some of her resolve and needed another way out. She had been just too dependent on Pat. It may be time to accept Lady Moses offer.

As she climbed the stone outcropping, she spotted Lady Moses' cabin. Grey smoke, the same color as the weathered cabin, flowed out of the chimney. The windows were dark and she couldn't see inside but she could feel that Lady Moses was in the cabin. She caught her breath and slowly pulled her tired body up the steps and rapped on the door knowing that this was going to be a life-changing meeting.

The Exchange

"Come in," called a voice from the back of the cabin.

As she opened the door, a small ray of sunshine that peered though the corner of the dirty window shone on Bertha's face.

"I knowed it was you. You came back, jest as I said you would. So whatja want?"

Somehow Bertha knew that Lady Moses already knew the answer but she took the next two hours explaining her plight. She ended by saying, "I never got to tell Pat goodbye and give him a proper burial."

"That's all well and good but whatja want me to do about it?"

Bertha hated this question. She had spent most of her life not really needing anything and certainly wasn't accustomed to asking strangers for help. But Lady Moses wasn't exactly a stranger. Clearing her throat she said, "I was hoping that you could take what I brought and do something for me."

"Well, spit it out child, I ain't gittin' no younger waitin' on you."

Bertha was momentarily amused that she was being called a child. But realizing she was half of Lady Moses' age, it was probably appropriate.

She grabbed her sack and poured out the contents in front of Lady Moses.

"Well that's a queer combination that requires some 'splainin'. I know the sang but what is this 'traption?"

"That's Pat's peg leg. It's the only thing I have left of him."

"I see. You know this is really gonna cost ya."

"I know."

"Well let's git to it. I'ma gonna give ya scrip for the ginseng so you can buy what you need for the kids."

She took her walking stick and pointed to get Bertha to pull some Mason jars off the shelf.

A pinch at a time, Lady Moses sprinkled powders over the ginseng and then waved the walking stick over it and mumbled some strange sounding words. A smoke formed and the roots began changing position. When the smoke cleared, they had formed the numbers 675.

76

"You accept the deal?"

Bertha nodded in agreement.

Suddenly more smoke formed and the peg leg moved to the coal stove and stood upright. Moments later Pat stood in front of Bertha.

Although their time was short, Bertha was able to say her goodbye to Pat.

She left the mountain that evening with Lady Moses saying, "Next time you come, you will be me."

Bertha provided for the kids and never returned to the mountain...until she died....when she was six and three quarter decades old.

That was when my brother was six and three quarter years old.

Sure enough, my granny returned to the mountain and the local folk say that Lady Moses looks a little younger these days.

Wolf
W. M. D.

1963 in the Appalachian Mountains

A dog barked in the background as the taupe haired boys played down by the creek with not a care in the world. The sun shone down on their backs ever gently, tanning their fair skin and bleaching their hair.

The boys were poor but they never knew it. They ran free though the woods, mountains and creek beds. They had a clean pair of cut off shorts and t-shirt everyday.

One day their dad brought home a stray dog. But for all the boys knew, it was a purebred. But its coloring betrayed its origin. The boys knew the dog was not a dog at all, but a wolf.

The Next Morning

They had escaped from their mother's eye to play for the day and all the joy that it provided. Never knowing there was a different world just beyond, their world was full of hope and adventure contained within the crevice of the mountains and streams.

The creek ran to the river where the bigger fish were.

The washtub that they pulled out of the old washing machine was now deeply embedded in the creek. The creek was inhabited with crawfish just beneath the mud if you were willing to dig for them. The minnow trap was sitting in the creek baited with a soured corn cob. The washtub served as a new habitat, a protected environment, for the 'crawdads' and minnows that represented a life filled with adventure and bigger fish to come. But only if they could escape the protection of the washtub.

Just up the hill, the railroad tracks were silent. Trains came and left from this point. For travelers, it was the beginning to an end. An end from whence they came never again knowing where they began.

The world where they lived was sheltered.

They had not a care outside its borders because their world was where the family lived.

All the neighbors were friends and there was no fear to be had. Until.....

The night was dark. The moon shone brightly.

A howl of an animal ripped through the quiet of the crisp night.

The boys counted the sound just as they had with finding the distance to a lightening strike and the sound of thunder. They figured the wolf was at least three miles away. Still, it was unsettling and they ran as hard as they could. The door slammed and their backs pressed against the door to hold back any evil that lay beyond the door.

"What the hell are you doing up? Get your ass to bed before I have to beat it." bellowed their dad. The boys scurried off to their bunk beds and covered their heads to ensure no evil could enter.

Their dad would never be found on the cover of Good Housekeeping or nominated for the "Greatest Dad." He pressed the boys to be better in every way and sometimes it included feeling the two-inch miner's belt. Still, the boys did love him. After all, you love your Dad because he loves you...no matter what.

As the weather transformed to a cool fall blanket, the trees mutated to reds and yellows and brightened the landscape. Soon the black walnut tree would lose the 2 ½ inch bombs from its branches. Jeff and Julius would run playfully under the tree shaking the branches as the bombs would fall. Occasionally, a bomb would hit them and leave a streak of green from the hull of the nut. It was one of their favorite times of the year.

After a few weeks with the bombs on the ground, Jeff and Julius were sent over to collect the bombs. The black walnut hulls were now somewhat mushy. As Julius picked up the bombs and threw them in the paper grocery bag, the pigment from the green hulls left a stain on his hands and on the bags. Over the next two weeks, they would return with 21 bags of bombs. Finally, their dad gave them their next task...pull off the deteriorating hulls and put the nuts in another grocery bag. It seemed as though it was taking months to do the chore, especially when the fall weather was calling to play football.

"Can we go play football?" asked Jeff.

"Finish two more bags and then you can go," said their dad.

The next two weeks were grueling for the boys. Their task was to break open the shell and pull out the nut and put it in a jar. With both hands on a hammer and the nut sitting squarely below on the concrete floor, Julius brought the face of the hammer in contact with the shell. The shell broke but only about a quarter of the shell broke away. Several more swings and finally the nut was open and the meat was in the jar that previously held peanut butter. Julius yelled, "Jeff, how many nuts are in two bags?" "I reckon about two million," Jeff called back. "We'll never get out of here!"

Football was freeing. The boys imagined themselves playing for their favorite teams, the Minnesota Vikings and the LA Rams. The cool, crisp air seemed to fuel the boys as they ran hard down the field throwing the football along the way. With a football in hand, there was never a fear. They played the rest of the afternoon and then headed home ready for supper.

When they reached the house, there was a commotion and the boys were sent back outside to play. It was close to dark and the boys had never been sent out to play at that late hour. Normally, they would eat supper and be sent to bed. But still, being outside was always better than being inside with the grownups

The night was darker than most. The moon was not visible nor were the stars. It was creepy. The air was not moving and there was a stench in the air that hung like a cloud. In the distance, they heard a wolf howl.

Grabbing a flashlight, they ran across the street and got Phillip to come out to play. Flashlight tag was the game and it seemed to go on all night. This was the first time that the boys had been able to play past midnight. The three boys heard the wolf howl for the third time and ran back home as fast as they could.

When they reached their respective homes, their mothers greeted them with hugs and swept them off to bed. They lay in their bed so exhausted they we too tired to eat and quickly fell asleep.

The next morning, there was something strange going on and they seemed to be kept from going to the living room. But it didn't matter, it was Saturday and they ran as fast as they could to the creek to look at the minnow traps. Sure enough, as they opened the two traps, there were at least three handfuls of minnows in each trap. They quickly transferred the minnows to the washtub. There was going to be great fishing ahead. They reset the traps with soured corn cobs.

All of a sudden, they heard a wolf howl and this time it sounded closer. This time, Wolf, their 6-month-old dog, began to bark. But even more strange was that the current of the creek seemed to change. There was almost a bow wave and to their amazement, they witnessed what seemed like hundreds of fish, jump across the washtub and back into the water.

Then a piercing voice yelled "J-e-s-s-eeeeeeee ! ! ! !"

Jesse knew that voice although he had not heard it in a very long time. Jesse ran as fast as he could up the hillside to greet his cousins. When Jesse and Julius got to the top of the hill, there stood their Uncle Eldon, Aunt Jill, and cousins Paul, Robert and Lee beside the green Pontiac.

A few minutes later Uncle Jack, Aunt Louise and cousin Pat pulled up in the Buick.

Why was everyone here? It wasn't Thanksgiving or Christmas.

Again, they heard the wolf howl in the background. But Jesse and Julius were the only ones that could hear it.

Died? Someone had died? Who?

Jesse and Julius had never known anyone who had died. They had killed their share of bugs, fish and even a squirrel or two but no one they knew had ever died….until now.

The casket was in the living room and chairs were set around the room but the kids were not allowed to go in. People had been coming through the house all day. Every one of them brought food; fried chicken, ham, potato salad, green beans, potatoes, biscuits, cakes, pies and sweet tea. Jesse and Julius had never seen so many people wearing nice clothes. Nor had they ever seen so much food, which was a welcomed sight, and they quickly devoured more than their share.

The visitors kept coming but all of them were so quiet and only spoke in whispers. They all seemed nice but very old. But still, the patting on the head by strangers was getting annoying.

Around noon, their cousins arrived to save the day. Time to run out and play.

After a full day of playing, they headed back to the house. There was still plenty of food. Then the boys heard the exciting news. Their cousins were spending the night. There were no hotels in the small town so everyone had to pile up into rooms and sleep on the floor.

Naturally, with twelve kids in the house there was plenty of horseplay. Finally as the smaller cousins fell to sleep, the older kids talked about the casket.

"Why won't they let us in the living room?" Julius said.

"Cause, they don't want us to see the body," replied Jesse.

"Why don't we go sneak in there right now?"

"Yeah, let's do it."

So creeping through the house the four older cousins began their adventure. They made it out the bedroom door and half way down the hall. The light from the moon cast a strange shadow on the picture of the Virgin Mary and her eyes seemed to follow them as they crept by trying to be silent. A howling wolf broke the silence and they scampered back to the bedroom and hid under the covers.

The same scene continued for the next three days; visitors coming through the house and kids being turned away from the living room and the almost ritualistic patting on the head. They told stories of Granny's life that everyone seemed to enjoy. Occasionally, someone would come in and play a church song on the piano and even when there was no one to play the piano, there was always someone singing broken verses of 'Amazing Grace'.

On the third night, Jesse was determined to lead his army to the living room. The four kids waited till everyone else was asleep and made their way down the hallway past the picture of the Virgin Mary. Even though her eyes followed them, they had enough courage to look away and move forward. Quietly they made it to the living room and there the casket was placed squarely in the middle of the room. They stood there almost frozen wondering what to do next. Eventually, they got up enough courage to walk up and touch the casket. A howl of the wolf quickly sent them scurrying back to the bedroom.

In the morning, their mothers woke them for breakfast and made them get dressed in their fancy clothes. After they ate, the younger cousins were sent off. Jesse, Julius and the older cousins were taken by the hand and escorted into the living room. This time, the casket was open.

"OK, it's time to say goodbye to Granny."

One by one, the cousins were lifted up to kiss Granny goodbye.

The living room was never the same. It was actually the dead room to Jesse and Julius, with the moving eyes of the Virgin Mary watching them.

The wolf howled.

Up in the Holler
Renee Haddix

I've always lived in the Appalachian Mountains. Tucked away in between the rolling green hills and fresh cold mountain rivers. In the summer time all you can see is green, green trees, and green grass.

Growing up out in the country, the only thing that hit the bottom of my feet was grass and dirt. I kicked my shoes off on the last day of school and only put them on when my mama would make me go to Sunday school. My shoes were back off before the doors on our old beat up station wagon were even shut. Then, we would putt around the twisty curves and up and down the hills, into the old holler.

I never knew why it was called the Holler, but I knew that it was scary at night. I use to lay in the very back and watch the stars out of the huge back glass windows in those old wagons. Once we hit that dark holler heavy with trees, I just knew that the tree branches were going to come to life and just snatch me right out of there. And, oh Lord, once

I saw *The Legend of Sleepy Hollow*, I was always so certain, completely positive, that the horse with the red glowing eyes with the headless man on his back, was running right next to us, waiting for us to have to stop for a deer to cross the road in front of us, to throw his fireball pumpkin head and catch us on fire. I had myself so convinced of this, that I could hear the hoof prints galloping right behind us. From then on I would squeeze up front between my Mama and Jenny. That ended my star gazing out the hatch of those old beat up station wagons.

I always wanted to believe that Mom bought those huge ugly old station wagons just to torture me, since I think we owned about ten in the whole eighteen years I lived at home, but in reality it was because we had a big old "Nothing but the blood," God-fearing family. There were eight of us in our family. Of course, there was Mom, Dad, Jenny, Tink, Will, Annie, Renee (that's me) and my little nephew Joe. Joe is Jenny's son, that she had way too early, but boy, am I ever glad that she did. Being the youngest of five was so boring. Annie wasn't sure she liked me at all, Tink and Will were already half grown. So when my new playmate came along, I was the happiest I'd ever been. He was always the perfect little fellow. I could talk him into about anything as long as I promised some playtime with his Matchbox cars. I'm sad to say though, there were times I didn't play with his stupid ol' cars because that was for boys.

Up that long Holler, we lived in a little white box house that only had two bedrooms in it, one tiny bathroom, a living room and a kitchen and that's all the room for the eight of us there was. We all had to share beds and covers at night. The plus side to that was getting into a warm bed on cold winter nights. Many nights the frost was so thick on the windows that you couldn't see the stars. I'd cuddle up with my sisters, getting ever so snug and warm. Annie often had no patience for my little ice cold feet trying to find a warm spot under her back. She was always smacking my butt and moving me away, but that didn't deter me, I was persistent. Finally she would give in and cuddle with me. I still miss that feeling. Nothing like sisterly love.

One of the first Christmases I can remember was in that little old house up the holler. I was probably about five years old and my big brothers were getting ready to trudge through about a foot of snow to cut down a pine off our neighbors' land so that we could decorate it. I remember asking Mom if I could go with the boys, expecting a "no" like the year before. I was completely taken by surprise when she said yes! So, Mom and Jenny bundled me all up, with grocery bags over my hand-me down shoes and socks on my little cold hands to go with my brothers, Tink and Will.

I remember the short little drive down the snow-covered road and just past our favorite swimming hole. We came to a stop just beside a barbwire fence. Tink scooped me up and over the fence and set me back into the deep snow. We trudged through the field of what looked like perfect Christmas trees, the icy snow crunching under our feet, for what seemed like an eternity. Tink walked ahead, swinging the axe that he would soon be using to cut down the unsuspecting tree. I remember how the metal would glint in the sun if he moved it just right. Will held my hand and talked to me about the trees and Christmas. Finally we stopped by the tree that seemed to be perfect for us, at least in the eyes of two teenage boys. It was a great big pine that I knew was way too big to fit in our little box house, but the boys were determined. They decided they would cut out the very top six feet of the tree. I remember how the axe sounded, with its *whacks* against the tree. Finally, after taking turns, the great pine fell. It was destined to be adored and decorated by a family that had nothing but love that Christmas. There was always love.

Mom and Dad both worked, so, during the summer, there were many days that it was just us kids. Jenny always managed to watch us well. Well, "well enough" anyway. We were hers for her bidding. We didn't dare argue too much for the fear of her yanking our tongues out with an old rusty pair of pliers. And if you haven't caught on yet, I have a rather great imagination. So I won't tell you what my five year old little mind thought when she DID do it to Annie for back talking her. In my eyes, Jenny was always the strongest and smartest of all of us. She always knew just when to hold my hand.

Summertime meant that there was no godforsaken school, no hour-long bus rides across bumpy dirt roads that often felt like it was gonna make me puke all over the place. One time, I did just that. Poor Annie had to clean it up, because old Eb, had a weak stomach. Let me tell you one thing, I never once lived that one down.

Summertime also meant that me and my sidekick, Fish Pole Joe, had all the time in the world to play and explore in the creek next to us. We used to catch tadpoles and just watch them for hours, thinking that we would see them sprout a leg right before our very eyes. Once we discovered that a tree had fallen once through the winter, and by summer we were able to use it as a bridge to cross into the meadow next to us.

One day, while we were playing, we decided to cross to the other side, so on our knees and hands we went, being careful not to fall. But even with all the precautions a six year old and a three year old could use, one of us still managed to fall in. Half way across our forsaken bridge, I looked down into the rock-filled water and, much to my horrifying discovery, there was a slew of water snakes swimming below us. But in my mind, they were gigantic rattlesnakes just ready to jump the seven-foot gap between us and devour me and Joe. I was absolutely certain that, before anyone would even miss us for gone, we'd be dead and lying in the shallow waters of Teter Creek. Of course, that's not what happened at all, but I did startle poor little Fish Pole Joe so badly that he fell off of our tree bridge, into the snake infested creek bed below. I never ran so fast nor yelled so loud for my big sister, Jenny to come rescue her poor boy, who I thought was dying with rattlesnakes attached to him. Needless to say that ended the tree bridge experiences that summer.

The next summer, another year older, and full inch taller, four year old Fish Pole Joe thought that he was a great raccoon hunter, and set out on his own up into the deep thick woods across from our home. He had taken Dad's coonhound with him. He was going coon hunting. The family hunted hours for him, while my stomach stayed in knots. I could only envision him being eaten by a big black bear or a ferocious mountain lion. Finally, just before complete dark set in, they found him. Sitting beside Joe was our good faithful dog, Jack, a slayer of many raccoons, but a guardian to one curious four-year-old boy. That day, I found the love that I have for dogs I still have to this very day. I also learned to keep a better eye out for my little playmate.

Later on that year, we moved out of the little box house. We said our goodbyes to the Holler, leaving it behind; along with the sad, small house, trading it for memories that would last a lifetime.

To Bill M., Address: In Glory

Marion Kee

Dear Bill,

Dropped by your homeplace, week before Thanksgiving, and nobody was t'home. I parked me down the road a piece and walked up, since perhaps they wasn't expecting company--nary a dog come out to bark. I don't believe your folks done sold the place, the family name's all over it, but it was quiet as the grave. Peculiar. Gone visiting, perhaps.

Be that as it may, somebody's taking care of the house. The windows was sparkling clear, I seen all the beds was made, the quilts was smoothed, the floors was spotless. And the hearth clean as milkweed silk. Not a wisp of smoke and the sun already lowering on the ridge.

They say the music still lives in them boards, and if you choose your time just right, you can hear it. I stopped up on the porch to listen, but all's I heard was the wind coming up in the trees. Kind of spooky-like.

I knocked and no-one came, and the door it was locked tight. Well, I reckon you got to do that on the Rosine Road, 'specially nowadays. So I walked around the place for a spell, and seen the henhouse tidy as you please and the chicken wire all shiny--not a hen to be found. No hogs in the pen neither, and frankly that might of been a good thing as by this time of year they'd of busted right out at that thinnest rail, low down. But it ain't broke. Why there's such a puny rail there anyways, I couldn't tell you. I figure your people would know better. By the look of them weeds inside, they didn't have no hogs this year to remind 'em.

Bill, there ain't no outhouse now, neither, and I'm a-thinking perhaps the County Health people come up there once too often and made your folks take it out. Looks like the well ain't got much use of late, the bail was laying up on top of the well-cover and dry as a bone--but then, it were a right sunny day. No bucket setting around, neither. So, I told myself they must of got one of them modern electrical pumps so's everything's been buried, but with all them windows the house has got, you can see plain as day they ain't put in a bathroom.

Now, I ain't one to judge what folks decide about their own property. But seemed to me like something weren't quite right, and it set me to worrying.

So I thought I'd just clear my head and walk out to Jerusalem Ridge afore I left, taking your advice that it's the most beautiful spot on God's green earth and I ain't never seen it yet. Then right away going out that road I slipped on something round and then t'other foot, too, and dang if it weren't a mess of black walnuts right there under the leaves, all stages of soft hulls. Been there a while, by the look of things. Right past the henhouse--a four-year-old could of been sent to pick 'em up, that close to home.

Well, that made the hairs stand up on my neck. Your folks ain't just stepped out, they ain't been gathering their own nuts, leastwise not in weeks. I sure hope nothing bad has got to them, but the more I slipped around on them hulls, with that there black-walnut smell a-rising up, the spooked-er I got. Then my feet decided I ought to get out and get gone while I still could.

So Bill, I hope you'll forgive me but I hightailed it back to my truck. I peeled out and got me down that hill to the hard road and you know it was an odd thing but there's a sign down there says the gate gets closed at five o'clock. It being ten of, I didn't wait around to find out what THAT was all about.

I know you're doing great where you're at now, and I ain't wishing you back even though this "New Grass" surely could use some straightening out. I just thought you ought to know. I figure you've got friends in High Places, might be able to check on your folks for you. Wherever they've wandered off to.

Signed,

An admirer

Flashes
Lee Keene

Half a Suit

We were going Christmas shopping, but it was too early for Santa to be in G. C. Murphy's. Mom promised we would go again after he arrived in town. We only had one vehicle, Dad was at work in the mine, and mom didn't drive, anyhow. My aunt picked us up. On the way, we stopped at the Post Office to get the mail. I was in awe of the very adult action of turning the little knob on the post box in just the right combination to open it. AB-D-E. At just shy of five years old, I had already memorized it.

There was no open counter, but rather a window to the back office, with black bars that could be pulled down when closed. We did not see the postmistress, but, just as we were about to leave, we heard her scream. My aunt ran to the window and stuck in her head.

"What's wrong? Hazel, what's wrong?"

The postmistress's head appeared in the opening. "They've shot the president! They've shot the president, in Dallas!"

A second of stunned silence, then, "Is he...gone?"

"I don't know. They just announced it." She disappeared for a moment and we heard the small radio's volume increase to it's maximum. Mom squeezed my hand so tightly I said "Ow!" and pulled away, but she grabbed it back.

Not satisfied with the lack of updates from the radio, Mom and my aunt decided to go home and watch television instead. A few people had gathered on the sidewalk outside the Post Office, abuzz with questions. Have you heard? Anything new? It was the Russians, I know it. Who else was hit? Not Jackie?

The short trip home was mostly silent, since my aunt's car did not have a radio. We went to the living room and turned on the Philco without having taken off our coats. Mom poked up the coal stove while we waited for the set to warm up and show us a picture.

The president was dead. Mom and my aunt cried. It was the first time I had seen it.

Dad, of course, already knew when he got home, even though our truck also didn't have a radio. Many years later, Dad told me he had heard the super say, "Serves the son of a bitch right." Dad was old and feeble by that time, but said, "I wanted to hit him."

I had to be quiet playing and not run around over the next few days, though I didn't understand why my pretending to be a cowboy would make a difference to the dead president.

When the funeral day came, the entire neighbor family, all ten of them, came to watch it on our television, since they did not have one. Even though Mom brought in the chromed-legged chairs from the kitchen table, they all turned them down and sat on the floor.

That night, I had a nightmare and woke up crying. I had dreamed of the president, shut up in a coffin, with the sound of dirt begin shoveled onto the top. In my dream, he was wearing pants, but no shirt. It took more than a half-century for me to understand that part of the dream. It just came to me in the shower one day, long after Dad was gone.

Dad never wore a tie, much less a suit. If Mom ever suggested it, Dad would say, "I ain't wearing no suit. There's no use wearing one until you die, and then they only put you in half of one."

I had misunderstood which half of the suit he meant.

Grapevine Sex

The Japanese beetles ate some leaves so completely that only the delicate filigree of veins remained, like ancient old lace doilies once belonging to a long-dead relative, pressed out in a Bible, brown and brittle with age.

"Damn things," Dad said. "I don't know why they ever brought them over here."

"Who brought them over here, Daddy?"

"The Japanese, I guess."

I was sent to the grape arbor every day to squash them, first between small, flat rocks, but later with two pieces of wood connected by a hinge and spring, like an oversized clothespin, that Dad had made for me. But, Dad had a less messy method.

"How come that beetle's on top of the other one, Daddy? I see them like that all the time."

"Uh. Well, they, ah, don't see too good, and just climb over one another instead of walking around. And they stop to rest. That's it. And here's what they get."

I saw particular satisfaction in Dad's face as he flicked the offending amorous beetle couple into his little jar of kerosene.

"Remember that," he said.

Going Somewhere

I combed my hair, or Mom did, after I took a bath. The oblong galvanized tub hung on a nail on the back porch when it wasn't being used. At bath time, it was pulled into a small room beside the kitchen and Mom poured hot water into it from a teakettle on the Warm Morning stove. Sometimes, if both of us needed a bath at the same time, my older brother would take his first, and mine would be taken in his leftover bath water, "warmed up" with another kettle that heated while he bathed.

But, sometimes, if we went somewhere on weekends, Mom would tell Dad to comb my hair as he was doing his own. In those days, we used hair oil or cream. Dad complained that he preferred Lucky Tiger, but "they don't make it no more, I guess." After that, he switched to

Brylcreem, and sang *"A Little Dab will Do Ya"* as he swept up his own pompadour.

He knew what came next, though. "Come here," he would say, already gruff in preparation. I would start to whimper, "I want Mom to do it."

"Com*eer*!"

I knew he meant business.

He squirted a small bit of the white cream into one hand and rubbed his palms together. Then, with both hands, he vigorously rubbed my head all over for an interminable time, making sure each shaft was coated with the essence before pulling the Ajax Unbreakable Under Normal Use pocket comb with two missing teeth roughly over my scalp.

"I don't know what you cry about every time I comb your hair."

As I got older, we never felt it necessary to discuss why getting my hair combed had been traumatic. Dad worked in low coal, usually twenty-eight inches. His hands (and, for that matter his knees) were covered with a half-inch of callous, rougher and tougher than the rawhide chew bones found in today's pet shops. Try rubbing one of those over a four-year-old's head.

First Day of Squirrel Season

Dad always liked to go squirrel hunting on my grandparents' farm on the first day of the season, and be in the woods before dawn. That meant leaving at 4:00 a.m. He, Mom, and I squeezed into the cab of his Chevrolet truck and rode almost fifty miles along curvy mountain roads, otherwise abandoned at that time of the morning. For the first several miles, I complained about being cold, because the truck needed a new thermostat. Since I rode in the middle, I held my feet tightly against the heater vent. When Dad lit a cigarette, he cracked his window, which just had the effect of pushing the smoke more rapidly in my direction.

92

"Just go to sleep," he said, when I complained.

I never could. I knew what the route looked like in the daylight, but it was different at night. Many of the houses could not be seen at all because they had no lights on. Some had a porch light, but the little pinpoint was all that was visible. I remember thinking, "I wonder what kind of people live behind that porch light? Are they the kind that, if we were in trouble, would come to our aid if we came knocking in the middle of the night?" I imagined scenes from old black-and-white movies I had seen, about strangers meeting and helping one another.

My grandparents heated with wood, and the smell of smoke hung in the foggy air as we arrived. Grandma always had breakfast ready. They made their own sausage, and that was the first 'inside smell' that struck us as we entered. After eating sausage and biscuits and apples, Dad and my uncles walked to the woods, and Mom and Grandma suggested that I lay on the couch with a blanket and go to sleep. There weren't many books at my grandparents' house, so I usually brought one with me.

"That's him," Mom would say. "Nose always stuck in a book."

"That's why he has to wear glasses," Grandma replied. "You let him read too much. It strained his eyes."

When the men returned, I had to help them clean the squirrels, gripping them by the legs while Dad peeled their skin inside out. Lunch was squirrel, its whitish gravy, and more biscuits and apples.

"I don't care how clean you pick it, there's always going to be a hair on squirrel," Grandma would inevitably say. She was right.

Driving back home in the afternoon, the hills would, in years with no drought or too much autumn wind, be ablaze with color. I took off my glasses off to blur them, thinking they looked like giant mounds of Trix cereal, something then new on the market that I occasionally nagged Mom into buying for me on payday.

"Put your glasses back on," Dad admonished when he noticed. "I don't want to have to pull over, with you getting carsick."

Today, when I smell sausage, I think of wood smoke and apples, and my grandparents' house. And, when I think of that, I think about the plastic cereal bowl and cup that sat on top of the pre-World War I era bureau in the dining room. The bowl was molded to look like a hollowed out log, and the cup was Woody Woodpecker, with his pointed head curving around to form the handle. I think it came to them free by sending in a number of Kellogg's Corn Flakes box tops. It sat there as a decoration, and an entire generation of my family looked at it with longing, wanting to ask to eat cereal out of it the way we had seen it done on the wavy-pictured black and white TV, but knowing better than to ask to do so.

I don't know whatever happened to that bowl and cup. They were probably thrown away after Grandma and Grandpa died. I would still like to have the chance to eat corn flakes out of it, and drink cocoa. Just once.

The Day in 1970 that Changed My Life

"That new station is supposed to be on tonight," Mom said while sat on the couch and snapped beans for the next morning's canning.

"What's supposed to be on it?" Dad asked. He was cleaning coal dirt from under his fingernails with a flat toothpick.

"School stuff, I think."

"Well, it better not cause no snow on the other two channels." He turned to me. "Y'all going to start watching television in school?"

"Ain't even got none," I said.

Mom told me to get up and change the channel to nine. "Might as well look," she said.

Arthur Fiedler's white hair danced as his arms flung back and forth, as the overture to *The Marriage of Figaro* possessed his body. The soaring music strained the Philco's tinny speaker.

"Turn it back," Dad snapped. "We ain't watching that stuff."

But it was already too late for me.

The Smell of Flowers

"You can't smell that?" Mom asked.

"Smell what?"

"Flowers."

"No."

"Nobody else ever can, I guess."

Grandma and Grandpa's house on the farm was a place where kids whispered and didn't run or track in dirt.

"Mommy had a baby that was born dead," Mom said. "It had measles. They broke out on the next day, after it was born. Undertakers came to the house back then, when I was a girl. The little coffin was set up right here, in the hallway. I helped pick the bouquet we put on top of it. Ever since then, whenever I come through here, I smell flowers."

I sniffed real big.

"Maybe," I said, hopefully. "I think I can."

"No. No, you can't."

Old Pictures

I was in junior high when we had to clean out Grandpa's house. It had set vacant for years, and Dad's brothers and sisters didn't help him pay the property taxes. It was near to falling down anyway. A black and white picture of John Kennedy and family coming out of church still hung on the bedroom wall, just where I had always seen it.

"We'll keep that," Dad said. "Unless they threw it out when they put Kennedy in, there's a picture of Roosevelt behind it. That's the one I always remember, growing up."

The frame was of rough wood, and seemed ancient. The corners had the remains of several tacks and screws used to hold it together over the years, and a piece of rusty wire stretched across the back.

The picture disappeared under a bed until a couple of years later, when we enclosed the front porch, and Dad, remembering it, thought he would bring it out to hang there. He put down newspaper and laid it on the kitchen table. "It'll fall apart if we hang it back up like that."

The old frame practically did so when he picked it up. The glass was cracked and came out in three sharp, pointed pieces. The back, a thin, warped piece of wood, splintered when Dad popped it out. The picture of the Kennedy family, more than a decade and a half old by then, turned out to be a campaign handout for a local politician hoping to ride JFK's coattails. The backing behind the picture was thicker than I imagined it to be, but I was anxious to see if the picture of FDR Dad remembered was still there.

"Here he is. This is what I remember." Dad peeled away the Kennedy picture, and the faded, smiling face of Franklin Roosevelt revealed itself. "Bout everybody we knew had one hanging somewhere," Dad said.

When he tried to dislodge Roosevelt, something else came along with it. Dad stuck his thumbnails into the corner, and pulled the backing off. Some of the ink hung on, leaving a blotchy picture of a stout man with a stark, roundish face.

"Dang," I said. "That's William McKinley. He was assassinated."

Dad scowled. "How old is that?"

"It was around 1900, about. That's how Teddy Roosevelt became president. So, about seventy-five years."

96

"Too bad it's not in better shape. I guess it got wet sometime. Probably a leak. If it's that old and Poppy had it, I guess it belonged to grandpaw way back then.

He turned the picture over. "Get me a thin knife. That one your mother peels potatoes with."

Dad took the paring knife and carefully worked it into the McKinley picture's corner. He peeled off another layer, with a sound like tearing a Kleenex.

"Hm. Look at that."

Little of the next picture's image remained, having stuck to the back of McKinley, but I could recognize the bearded figure.

"That's James Garfield. He was assassinated, too."

"Never heard of him. When?"

"Way back. Almost a hundred years ago. 1880s, I think."

"You *think*? That's why I send you to school."

"1880s.

"I guess grandpaw had that, too." He picked up the crumbling picture and peered intently at one corner. "There one more layer behind this one. What do you reckon it is?"

"I know what I hope it is!" I said, excitedly.

"Ain't none of these in good enough shape to be worth anything."

"I don't care. Can you peel it off?"

The final layer left even more of itself on the back of the previous, making it difficult to make out, but it finally slipped free.

"Well," Dad said. "Look at that."

My face fell as I saw a deteriorated mid-Victorian magazine page with a sketch of a little girl with flowing curls. I could just make out a few lines of cozy verse underneath it.

"Shoot," I said.

"What were you expecting?" Dad asked.

Them's Fancy People

I took them to Old Salem in North Carolina once, a couple of hours down I-77. It wasn't crowded that day, and they liked seeing the old tools and furniture, and I thought that, for something different and nice, I would buy them lunch at the on-site restaurant. It had a beautiful terrace in the back, covered in wisteria. Out of habit, they ordered the least expensive things on the menu.

"We should have just stopped at Hardees on the way back," Dad said, "instead of paying ten dollars for a sandwich."

The only other diners on the terrace were a smartly dressed young woman and an older, white-haired gentleman. He was wearing a crisp blue blazer and looked very distinguished. From snippets of conversation, I took it that the man and woman were not related, and did not know one another particularly well, their conversation peppered with questions.

When the waiter, an awkward young man who appeared to be trying really hard, brought them the wine list, the older gentleman asked several questions about the beverage offerings the waiter could not answer, causing the man to launch into an explanation meant, to me, to show his wide knowledge on the subject.

Making our way back to the Plymouth after we finished our sandwiches, Dad said, "Them was fancy people, there." He said it with no malice, or even judgment of any kind, much like "It's starting to rain," or "Jimmy bought a new tractor."

It caused me to wonder if he had, ever in his life, wanted to be one of them fancy people. People who wore blazers and knew about wine. How did one achieve it? Was it only by birth, or could it be learned? But, his placid acceptance of there being two kinds of people in America disturbed me most.

Slow Children

When Dad got old, I took him to his doctor's appointments. On the way back from one, we passed a sign that said, "SLOW Children Playing."

"That's a pretty good idea," I said.

"What is?"

"Putting up signs like that in neighborhoods where there are kids who aren't too smart. They're kind of slow. They might not think twice about running out into the road. You've got to be careful."

"Oh. I didn't rightly know that's what it meant, I guess."

He didn't see me grin.

After a while, he said, "That nurse had me fill a cup, and gave me one of them little alcohol patches in a package. She told me to use that to wipe it. I wondered about that. Don't know what it was to her. But it just hit me. Reckon she meant for me to wipe it *before* I went in the cup, instead of after?"

I was driving, so I will never know if he smiled.

Fishing, gone

A year or two after Dad died, I dreamed he and I went fishing at a place I hadn't been since I was a kid. The track down to the river was not really a road, but a rutted, muddy path. And Dad wasn't the man of my fishing youth. He was the grey skinned, 90-pound cancer victim he was during his last six months. We were in an old pickup truck I had once owned, and being tossed about the cab as we broached each crater in the path.

When we finally reached the river, there was a smooth green lawn and picnic shelter, something that never actually existed at the place. Dad got out of the truck and held onto it for support with skeletal arms.

"Where's the fishing rods? You didn't lose them, did you?"

The only thing in the bed of the truck was a cooler containing our lunch and drinks.

"They must have flipped out when we hit the last big hole. It's just up there. I'll run back and get them. They ain't lost."

"I hope not," he answered grimly.

I jogged back up the sort-of road, trying to skirt the large puddles that reached all the way from side to side on the slippery trace. I found the rods lying just where I expected them to be, and returned to the shelter.

Dad was hanging on to the bed of the truck, and the cooler sprawled open on the ground, its contents scattered over the wet grass. Dad was crying.

"I couldn't do it," he sobbed.

"Why didn't you wait for me?" I yelled.

"I thought I could do it, but I can't do nothing no more."

I woke up very sad, and I never dreamed about Dad again, at least that I remember. That was the only time I saw him cry.

100

Horse Creek
Lee Keene

"Through the grace of God, Amen. Oh, great friend and benefactor Columcille, I give to you a continuation of my report on the voyage of Breanainn of Clonfert, our mutual laborer in the vineyard of our Lord. I have, previously, relayed to you our adventures upon our journey to Eden, now known as Breanainn's Island.

How, under the Guidance of God, in the Year of Our Lord, 554, Breanainn chose fourteen monks to accompany him, and the Spirit moved him to include me into that number.

How, after prayer and fasting, we left Llancarfan Abbey and then the shores of Eire, discovering islands inhabited with Devils and Demons of All Sorts, and even mountains with direct vents to Hell, spewing forth fire and brimstone, creating great crystalline pillars standing in their wake.

How, after encountering great beasts and islands with plumes of water and slippery, living surface that sank upon our building of a fire, we came upon the Great Sinner Judas seated upon a rock, ashiver with wet and cold, having been given through the Mercy of God a reprieve from the torment of Hell during Sundays and Feast Days.

How, after finding lands of ice and of vines, and enduring the greatest hardship, we reached Eden and traveled deep into its interior, encountering beasts unseen by Man since Our Lord removed Adam and Eve for their transgressions.

How, along with the strange beasts and flora, we were given visions of strange lesser angels, perhaps still in formation and confined to Eden, naked and both male and female, and even infants at the breast. They viewed us with great curiosity, perhaps being aware of our kind before The Fall, but having been deprived of contact after Satan's treachery.

How, after traveling the rivers of gentle land, we tread great mountains, higher than any we had seen.

I will now relate to you how we left the mark of the Advent of Our Lord indelibly impressed upon the timeless firmament of Breanainn's Island.

After many days of perilous and most difficult travel, we followed a small but rapid stream through the mountains. Along it's banks, there were occasional broad, flat plots showing signs of having been inhabited and cultivated by the lesser angles. They did not, at that time, show themselves unto us, though their presence must have been quite recent.

Near the mid of day, Breanainn shielded his eyes from the sun and looked up toward Heaven, seeing a break in the verdant wall of green originally planted by Our Lord to feed his creation. He squinted at it, considered it, and then called his great friend and helpmate Malo, whom he had baptized upon the latter's denial of the pagan faith many years before, to his side. The two great men spoke in low tones, and then prayed together.

Upon rising, Breanainn raised his hands and boldly said, "The Lord has provided us a slate upon which to proclaim the Advent of Our Lord to this land, which has been cut off from the Church since the sin of our great father and mother generations ago. The Word has not been preached, and the land is not whole. We may never see Eire again, but we will not leave without leaving visible mark of the Son upon it." Malo nodded his head, eyes tightly closed, and whispered agreement.

We ascended the mountain toward the break in the flora with difficulty, the vines and undergrowth being thick, with towering trees unknown in Christendom the size of middling boats through the trunk. The objective proved to be a smooth vertical cliff of whitish stone, with the crusty, dry, grey moss abundant in that place clinging thickly across the face, well protected by an overhang that made a shallow cave. Breanainn set our brothers to scraping it off. When they had completed their task, he said to me, "Gobban, you among us have been blest with the skill of hammer and chisel. You are God's chosen to imprint the Good News of our Savior's birth upon this land, unwillingly abandoned by man as punishment for his weakness."

I set to work with hammer and chisel, while Breanainn gave me the words to incise. The stone was of exceeding hardness, causing some lines to not satisfy me in their straightness, but, over all, the result was quite edifying. Completing the work required staying at the cliff throughout the night, and, although Breanainn would have had me work by torchlight, fatigue overtook me and the sun was high the next day when the work was complete.

When I finished, Breanainn called the brothers together and read the inscription with great satisfaction:

'At the time of sunrise a ray grazes the notch on the left side on Christmas Day, a Feast Day of the church, the first season of the year. The season of the Blessed Advent of the Savior, Lord Christ. Behold He is born of Mary, a woman.'

We prayed a prayer of rejoicing before leaving that place, knowing that the Word would stand for eternity."

"Howard's got Pinnacle beat," Rodney said, pushing the butt of his third hotdog into his mouth.

"Bull," Sam snorted as he swirled a fry into a white paper container of ketchup. "If I had a car, I would drive over to Pineville every day for Pinnacle's."

"That's downright unpatriotic. Keep your business in Oceana. You don't want the local economy to falter, do you?"

Both teen boys laughed at the last statement and emptied the remnants of their lunch into a trashcan.

"I can't believe you've never hiked up there to see the Indian marks in that cave before. If it ain't playing video games, you have no interest in it."

"I guess that's why you're so bad at them, dweeb. You don't have my dedication. What has tromping up and down the hills ever gotten you?"

"Girls like the outdoors type," Sam replied, puffing out his chest.

"Now it's my turn to say bull!" Rodney retorted.

The banter continued as the boys walked through town and turned onto a side street toward the creek and railroad track. Sam, the more fit of the two, quickly mastered the gait necessary for efficient walking on the ties, while Rodney occasionally stumbled and uttered mild oaths.

"Up the hill, just up there. It's not far," Sam eventually said, sensing his friend was losing interest. The boys left the track and climbed the steep hillside, their progress slowed by multiflora rose.

"I hate this stuff," Rodney hissed as he pulled a cane of thorns from his shirtsleeve. "My grandpa said the government brought it here from China or somewhere, way back. He doesn't like the government much, anyhow."

"Right up here." Sam pointed toward an outcropping of sandstone with a substantial overhang, showing white against the green of the surrounding vegetation.

Partially out of breath, Rodney looked at the foot of the outcrop and motioned toward an empty vodka bottle with his head.

"I didn't know the Indians drank vodka."

"Well, I guess that ain't all they did. Look." Sam pointed to a wrinkled, used condom a few feet away.

"Aggh! Can you imagine doing it up here on the ground? Oh, I shouldn't say that. I bet you imagine exactly that all the time, Sam the Great Outdoorsman!"

"Don't complain about someone else's success. That's my motto."

104

"You're just glad that someone in Oceana ain't a git-none like us. It gives you something to strive for. And to think about while you're in the tub."

"Shut up." This time, there was an edge in Sam's voice. "Are you going to look at the Indian writing or not?"

The boys stepped into the shelter formed by the overhang. Rodney ran his hand over the series of line markings incised into the rock.

"Don't do that," Sam snapped.

"Why not?"

"They say oil or acid or something from you hand will make 'em wear away eventually."

"Yeah, like just touching them will make them wear away! You're dense. They've been here a thousand years, and my touching them will make them wear away."

"Well, if they don't mean nothing to you, let's go." Sam turned to leave.

"Wait a minute. I didn't say they weren't neat. Let me look closer. I won't touch them again, Miss Manners."

Rodney scanned the markings several times. "A thousand years old? I didn't know the Indians could write back then. Pretty cool, I guess."

"Yeah. Now you've seen them, you ready?"

"I'm ready. Thanks for bringing me. Really. I'll buy you an ice cream. I could use one after this walk."

"Benefactor Columcille, after our prayer, Breannain and Malo knelt and wrapped their arms around themselves, gently rocking, while the Spirit filled them. They fell into such a state often, being given revelation from The Lord. Malo came back to us first, shaking his head and rubbing his eyes. When Breannain rejoined us in this realm, Malo said to him, 'There is another place. Another sheltered tablet upon which to inscribe the Good News, a day's distance. Did you see it?'

'Yes, Malo, the Spirit revealed it to me as well. Follow the stream. We shall pass a place where it washes upon black rock, and we will look up and see the place. Gobban will again leave our mark,' Brennan said, extending his hand toward me.

'Yes, my brother, follow the stream. But something was revealed to me that I do not understand." Malo seemed troubled as he gave this statement.'

'Share it, Brother Malo.'

Malo seemed hesitant, but said, 'Follow the stream, as you said. But, something else, strange, not of our speech. Is it possible, Breannain, that the lesser Gods here have influenced the Spirit's guidance with their ancient knowledge and language? I heard, repeated, 'follow route eighty-five.'

I, and the rest of the brothers, was taken aback by the strange words, fearing Malo could have been processed by an unknown ancient spirit with a voice.

Breannain frowned, and said, 'Put it out of your mind, dear Brother. Follow the stream.'

In the Name of God, Amen, I shall continue my report to you, Columcille, upon the morrow."

Ed. note: The "Horse Creek Petroglyphs," rock-cut inscriptions found in a cliff face in Wyoming County, West Virginia, and similar markings in nearby Boone County, have been a subject of study and disagreement for years. They appear to date from the 6th – 8th centuries. The original settlers thought the glyphs had been made by the Native Americans, though they do not seem to match any known Native markings. They do, however, resemble an ancient Irish writing form known as Ogam, and more than one academic has conjectured that the fabled wanderings of Irish monks included present day southern West Virginia.

Last-sum
Lee Keene

I didn't have a regular job in high school. There weren't many around for Buckhannon-Upshur students in the 70s anyhow, and I didn't try hard enough, maybe. But I was a fill-in for just about everyone I knew. Whenever a teenager in the whole county needed somebody to work for him, or even her, so they could be off, I was there. I learned to do lots of different things that way. I was pumping gas once, like you did back then, in late September when a Cadillac with Pennsylvania tags pulled up. It had an older couple in it. The guy was wearing a Hawaiian shirt and the woman was as broad as a house. He reminded me to check the oil, clean all the windows, check the air, don't fill it until it splashed out, all those things.

When I finished up, the man asked me, "Son, where can I find some real hillbillies, without going off the highway much?"

"What do you mean?" I couldn't quite believe what I was hearing.

"You know. Like the tarpaper shacks and that kind of thing. Bad teeth. Like you see in the magazines during elections. I don't want to go up dirt roads with this car, though, if I can help it."

I paused a minute to see if he was about to break out in a laugh and give me a buck for listening to his joke, but he was serious. When I didn't answer, he said, "I take pictures. It's my hobby after I retired. I would like to get some pictures of real hillbillies, you know, like in the movies. Ma and Pa Kettle kind of stuff, or Peace Corps, even better."

"The Peace Corps is foreign, Sam," the broad woman said. "It's called something else with hillbillies. Vista, I think."

The man looked annoyed. "Same thing, Gail. So, you going to tell me where I can find them, or not?"

"Well, sir, I would like to help, but I'm afraid you're too late," I said, sincerely.

"Too late?" the man said with a scowl. "What do you mean? It's not even noon yet."

"No, sir, that's not what I mean. I mean too late in the year. Hillbillies are out of season now."

"Out of *season*? What are you talking about?"

"Well, sir, they all leave around the middle of August to go back to Pennsylvania and teach school."

I got other fill-in jobs pumping gas before I graduated, but no more at that station.

You might guess, I was a little bit of a talker back then. It got me in trouble some, but, looking back, I wouldn't have it any other way.

Now, my buddy Walsh was one of the teenagers who had a more regular job. I never could figure out why he could get one and I couldn't, except his dad was a professional type and mine wasn't. And he was better looking. Don't let anyone tell you those things don't make a difference. Anyway, it was after school and on weekends, for Reynolds Floral. He delivered flowers, using a 12-passenger Dodge van with all the seats but the front ones removed, and racks in the back to hold arrangements. Reynolds probably wouldn't like it if they had known I went with him sometimes, just for fun. I can't tell you how many times we pulled that van off the road and drank beer and listened to the radio while he was making his $2.50 an hour. Those were happy, happy times, until the music started changing to Disco that summer.

This one time in particular, Walsh picked me up when he was making a delivery. The route took us close to the house of one of the cheerleaders, whose family had more money than his, even. They had a pool, with a fence around it, and the rumor was that the girl, I won't name her name because she's a lawyer in Morgantown now, would swim naked, or at least lounge without a top on. So, we pulled that van around on an old logging road on the mountain above her house and parked, looking straight down on the pool. Walsh had binoculars, and I had "borrowed" the scope off my dad's 30.06, because I knew that, if there was anything to be seen, Walsh would hog the seeing of it.

There was not a thing to look at. Nobody in the back yard at all. Just water in a pool, with a couple of blow-up things floating in it. Between that and the Bee Gees on the radio becoming what they had become, I was pretty disappointed.

Walsh kept hoping she would come out, and waited longer than he should to get the late-order flowers to a funeral. He cussed the way you probably shouldn't when we got to the church and it was empty. Everybody had already left for the cemetery, way out in the country.

Walsh was grim while he drove, both from naked cheerleader disappointment and worry about his job, I guess, so I tried to cheer him up.

"Yep, Walsh, funerals are funny things, now. My dad grew up in one of the logging camps and he remembers the trouble they had burying people in the winter back then. This is a nice warm day for it, and they got end loaders and four-wheel-drive Suburbans for hearses if they need them, but not back then."

"Yeah? And I'm sure you know all about it, just like everything else, I guess." He was aggravated.

"Well, just what I'm told. And I read something more than Penthouse once in awhile. So there. Anyhow, when he was little, he went to a burying once way up on the mountain above the camp. They didn't waste good ground for cemeteries back then. There was two feet of snow; no horse and wagon or any of the old trucks they had back then could make it. It took everybody in the camp practically to trudge that coffin up the hill. And, just before they got to the top, two or three of them slipped at the same time and fell, and dropped that wooden box."

"Shut up. I like this song." He reached down and turned up the volume on *Jet Airliner* by the Steve Miller Band. Afterwards, *"Easy"* came on, Walsh cussed and turned it back down, and I went on.

"It slid all the way back down the mountain, with half the men and women of the community chasing after it. Wouldn't that have been a sight to see, Walsh?"

"Don't talk about sights to see, dip s---," he said. "I had my heart set on a sight to see."

I ignored him. "In fact, and Dad saw this with his own eyes, it slid all the way down the mountain, and right across the road through the middle of the camp, and straight into the door of the company store. Slid right inside."

"Did it now?"

"Yep. And the force jolted the lid open, and the corpse sat right up, as they will sometimes do. And do you know what it said, that corpse, to the store clerk?"

Walsh sighed. "No. I'm sure you're going to tell me."

"It said, 'Haven't you got anything to stop this damn coffin?' Coffin. Coughin'. Get it?"

"Bite me," Walsh said.

"Any chance this service will have a bagpiper, you think?" I asked.

"How should I know?"

"First time I heard one of them was at the Veterans' Day parade when I was a little kid. It scared me. I thought it was an ugly old woman being attacked by a giant spider. When I figured out who was hurting whom, I told him that it would quite screaming if he would stop squeezing it."

"Do you ever shut up?" Walsh asked.

110

"When I sleep. Or maybe not. Charlie said I talk in my sleep. At least I have the room to myself now that he got married. Some people have houses big enough to have their own rooms from the beginning, though, now don't they?"

"Well, some people go to college and get better jobs and can afford bigger houses. So, bite me." Walsh said that a lot. Later in life, I looked back and wondered if there was something Freudian about it. I didn't let it bother me.

"Funny thing, about bagpipes. There're lots of people who say they want them at their funeral, but never listen to them while they are alive. So, they only want to be around them when they can't actually *hear* them. But my aunt, she's a nurse's aid in Fairmont, told about an old guy who really loved them, though. He was dying in the hospital and didn't have any family at all, but she promised she would make sure he had bagpipes when he was buried. She is just that kind of person."

"I wish you were that kind of person," Walsh said.

"You mean, always wanting to help people, like my aunt?" Altruism, even as a suggestion to someone else, sounded strange coming from Walsh.

"No, like the old guy. Dying," Walsh smirked.

I didn't acknowledge it. "So, she finds out where the old guy was going to be buried, way out in the country somewhere, and hires a bagpiper to play at the graveside. She didn't give him very good directions. She's nice, but a little scatterbrained."

"So you get that pretty natural, I guess." Walsh was quick with that reply.

"Anyway, that bagpiper was all decked out in his kiltie and such, driving out in the country to find the burying, and got lost. Finally, he saw just two guys up on the hill with shovels and said, "Shoot, I've missed it already.' But he's determined the old guy would get what he wanted, plus he was making $25 on the deal, so he screeched up, jumped out, played *Amazing Grace*, and drove off. Mission accomplished. One of the guys with a shovel started to tear up, and said 'Jim Bob, that was the most beautiful thing I've ever seen.' And do you know what Jim Bob said?"

"I'm sure as hell not going to ask for it. I know you're going to tell me anyway." Walsh was right, of course.

"Old Jim Bob dabbed his eyes with his teary bandanna and said 'Sure 'nuff, Eugene, and I've never seen anybody have that kind of respect for a new septic tank before.'"

Walsh abandoned his usual 'Bite me" for something more colorful, but still, in retrospect, with possible Freudian overtones.

The cemetery was on a dirt road, with pasture and woods all around, and a barbed wire fence around it. I figured the graveside words might be over by the time we arrived, and there wouldn't be anything to do but pile the flowers on top of those already there after the gravediggers filled in the hole. But, when we pulled up and got out, it was plain it wasn't over. In fact, it hadn't begun.

About fifty people, all dressed up in their church clothes, stood around the grave, looking confused. I could tell which one was the preacher, because he had the biggest Bible, but he wasn't saying a word. Nobody was. The casket was on the ground beside the grave, and the vault was nearby. I couldn't quite figure it out.

Walsh saw it as a chance to at least get the flowers set up before the thing started, and we went right to work.

When we got close to the grave, though, we heard the most God-awful wail, coming from inside it. It caused everyone to start looking around, like they didn't want to make eye contact with anyone else, and pretend they didn't hear it.

"What *is* that?" Walsh hissed at me.

"Durn if I know," I said. "I guess we'll see in a minute."

He paused. "Let's set up the flowers and get out of here."

Nobody said a word to us as we carried the flowers up to the graveside. We looked in and saw it: a Holstein cow, standing pretty as you please, down in the grave. She didn't seem to be in any distress, but let out a bellow now and then to remind everyone she was there.

We hurried back into the van and drove off. Walsh spun a few gravels, which he shouldn't have done, but I doubt anyone noticed, given the circumstances.

Neither of us said anything for several minutes. Finally, I conjectured, "I guess it got through the fence last night and fell in without anyone knowing it until they all showed up today with the deceased. You've got to admit, we'll probably be pretty old before we see a more 'What now?' situation than that, man."

He reached down and turned the radio back on, right to the opening of *I'm Your Boogie Man.*

"Bite me," he said.

Ed. note: This piece, used here with permission of its author, originally appeared as part of three vignettes combined as "*3-Sum,*" published in *Mountain Mysts: Myths and Fantasies of the Appalachians* (P. Ray Lewis and Danny Kuhn, Ed. 2015 Headline Books, Terra Alta, West Virginia, 224 pp., available on Amazon.com*).*

Apotheosis: November 30, 1930

Lee Keene

Paul looked glum. "Today's the day, isn't it?"

"What's this?" Peter feigned surprise. "Here in 'world without end' you're concerned about the date, all of a sudden. What could bring this on? Thinking the boss might have made a mistake with this one?"

"You know better. He doesn't make mistakes."

Peter's black-tinged-with-grey beard broadened slightly with a grin. "And yet, you have worries and cares, when I thought we left all those behind. All over a little old lady."

"I have neither!" Paul snapped. "And I don't appreciate your questioning..."

"Relax! I said worries and cares. That doesn't mean you left your sense of humor behind as well. Get it out from under the bushel. I'm looking forward to it, myself."

"You would. You seem to appreciate...salty."

"Salty? Like a fisherman? Careful now." Peter's feigned surprise turned to feigned indignation.

"It's just that...do you really think she will fit in? Do you know how many people over the years she told to go to Hell?"

Peter's brow furrowed as he laid down his quill and flipped through the pages of the huge book in front of him, adjusting himself on his stool and running down lines of handwritten script with his finger. Finding the entry he sought, he said, "As a matter of fact, I do. And you know that I do. It's eight thousand, four hundred, and eighty-six."

Paul scowled with I-told-you-so satisfaction. "Hm. And where's the glory in *that*?"

114

Turning his attention again to the book, Peter said, "Well, for what's it worth, eight thousand, one hundred, and four of them *are* actually in Hell, so it wasn't exactly a false condemnation."

"But not all!" Paul was quick with his response.

"No, no, you're right. Not all." Peter paused for effect, and added, "Three hundred and two of them are *living*, so the jury is still out!"

Paul's voice was sharp as he interrupted Peter's laughter. "You know what we can expect now? Turmoil, where there should be none. People who don't know how good they have it, even here, with supreme benevolence, will begin to question. Maybe even want more, when there can be no more. Disruption. Malcontent. Questioning. Dissatisfaction. Looking at the different levels and mansions and rewards and demanding to know why they exist. Is *that* what you want? You're not exactly apart from management yourself, you know."

"Paul, my friend. My true friend. Think about what you just said. Did all that not describe us, once? Was it not the basis of our belief, the eternal truth? You know the answer. She will be fine. We all will. We need her, and she deserves us, or at least as much as any of us humans do. We all fall short, but she's a fighter. Like you and me."

Paul sighed, resigned. "Yes. I know. But she will make many uncomfortable."

A single raised eyebrow on Peter's face caused Paul to immediately regret his last statement.

"*Heaven* forbid *uncomfortable*, Paul."

A crowd had gathered at the gate during their conversation, and the two men turned when they heard a trumpet blast. "She's here. Courage my friend," Peter said with a sideways smile.

The crowd parted to allow the two to pass through as they walked toward the solitary figure of a stout old woman with white hair and a black dress covering every inch of her but face and hands.

"She will be so impressed with her glorified body in a moment," Peter whispered to Paul. "I always love that part."

'I'm sure she will check for the union label, so you had better see to it," Paul growled.

Peter pulled himself to his full height and announced, with gravity, "Mary Harris Jones." His countenance softened, and he looked at the old woman. "Mother. Mother Jones. Welcome."

Country Road
Paul Lubaczewski

Author's historical preface: Most of the historical land rushes in American history get taught in school to some degree: the African American flight to the north, the dust bowl flight to California, etc. One that gets rarely mentioned is the flight from Appalachia, in the 1950s, and even continuing now. By the mid-50s, with new industrial techniques, mining employment in Appalachia began to plummet. Today in all of West Virginia there are only twenty-three thousand or so employed in mining and mining related fields. McDowell County West Virginia got hit the hardest; it went from a peak population of one-hundred thousand to two-hundred fifty thousand souls in the early 1940s, to less then twenty thousand today. The people left to follow the work, leaving their homes, sometimes with most of the belongings still inside, hoping to come back one day. Often they were the descendents of the original Scotch Irish settlers whose families had been there for centuries in their hollows and on their mountains. The Utah Phillips song *"The Green Rolling Hills Of West Virginia"* is about the migration. All through McDowell County, the homes they left sit abandoned and empty.

REGARD

An empty building. An old building. A *truly* empty building, one that has seen neither life nor maintenance for many years. Light leaks

116

through a windowpane, literally leaking through because of the grime and the grit of the years without a rag to wipe it clean.

The moon has come up over the mountains, illuminating the world with its glow and reflected light. Dust and grime aside, the ghost of the sun has found its way through a remaining pane of glass in to this empty house.

It shines diffused on a little doll in the windowsill. A little kewpie curio doll, the sort they used to give away at carnivals, all pixie cherub cheeks and a perfect little knowing smile. If it had known that the grime of the abandoned house was going to be falling on it for all these years, maybe it wouldn't have been smiling so much the day it was made?

The light reflects dimly off its frozen smile.

REGARD

Sarah had been crying all day. In fact, she had been crying for days on end. It was all so painfully *unfair*. Her mother had long since given up on cleaning off her tear streaked face until bath time, it had been such a constant, and the poor women had troubles enough to be sure. She loved her little girl, but sometimes you just have to let them cry it out.

Sometimes you just can't wave your hands and fix anything. You can only help them deal with their reality, and find the pieces for them to pick up.

Sarah sat on the steps with her dog Jebadiah, who attempted to lick her face clean in a brief moment of respite from wailing. Sarah looked at him and started to snivel again. Jebadiah was one of the many things for which she shed her tears. She wanted him with her, but the sight of him just broke her heart all the more. Jebadiah may be her dog today, but he wouldn't be tomorrow.

He'd be staying. Sarah and her family wouldn't.

It'd started half a year ago. Her Daddy had come home sad faced. While Sarah lay in bed she could hear her parents talking, it seemed like they'd never stop. She couldn't make out the words through the thick wood floor.

Oddly enough, for a few months things seemed normal, if not a little melancholy, around the house. But then one day after supper Daddy announced that they'd have to cut back on few things, as they were going to getting relief checks for a while. This sounded confusing, getting something sounded like having more, not less. A few days later she mentioned it to a classmate, Jimmy Fletcher, at her little country school, and he responded by saying "Your Pa too huh? The mine laid a lot of people off."

This took some further asking around to get the full story (little girls should know their place, and not ask their parents their business). The mine where her father and a lot of the other men in town worked had run out. The vein of coal they were following just wasn't safe to keep chasing anymore. Other mines were starting up, so most of the men were applying and hoping they'd be hired on at them.

But it soon became apparent that these mines were more modern, and would never hire on all the men in town who'd been put out of work. A few were hired up immediately, some were told to wait and see. It all seemed to go by seniority and closeness to retirement and all. As the waiting drug on though, more and more families just left.

Empty houses lined the streets where once Sarah could have found a half a dozen playmates.

Empty houses were all that was left of all the people. Abandoned shells.

Just the mountains of her home, and no one to share them with

118

A week ago Sarah was finally told, they'd be leaving their empty shell behind too.

And that's when the crying started.

Through bleary eyes, alone on the porch with Jeb, she saw her father approaching, and she knew why. But she didn't want to go, everything she knew, everything she wanted out of life was there in the mountains. She had never wanted to leave. Even visiting relatives had seemed a chore one did for politeness.

"I got to take him Sarah, he can't come with us. Mister Ravelli's waiting. It was nice enough for him to take him in, and we can't let the man wait any longer."

And then Sarah was alone, with her steps and her tears, not even a dog for company.

Later, when a shadow fell over her downcast view of the steps, she knew it was her Pa, but she was mad and sad enough that she wasn't going to acknowledge his presence without more provocation then a mere shadow.

"Pumpkin," her father started, "still mad, huh?"

She nodded quickly and hotly, not looking at him.

She could hear his sigh of resignation before he continued, "Look. I've told you, I've been hired on up in Pennsylvania at a mill, and we gotta go where the work is."

For this his reward was only more sad, mad silence. He took her chin in his calloused hand and made her look at him before he said, "Look I don't know if I've said this before, or even if I'm going to say it *right,* now, but I want you to listen to me. I *have* to look after you and your Mom, Pumpkin. It is my job as you're daddy. It's what all daddies do. Why, my daddy's daddy brought our family here in the first place. But times have changed, sweetie. The world's changed, the mine is played out, and the new ones don't need so many men."

He paused not for effect as much to compose his next set of thoughts before recommencing, "I can see already, there's going to be a world of possibilities for you. As smart as your momma surely is, ones she would have never dreamed of, you can have. You can be something more than us some day. But one thing's for sure, you won't get there, wherever there is, sitting here in these hidden mountains, collecting no damned relief checks for the rest of your life. You understand me girl?"

The response was another cursory sullen nod.

Her father sat down on the step in the spot just recently vacated by Jebadiah. He sat for a while in deep contemplation, while being angrily ignored by his little girl. Finally, in a quiet voice, husky with his middle age, "Alright girl, let's see if this helps, I'm gonna show you a bit of mountain magic, but it only works if you really believe in it. That little doll thing you won at the fair, you know the one. You have it with you most of the time. Go get it, and you get it now before we have to leave."

She stared at him surprised for a moment. Shaking herself free from his hand, she darted for the car out in the drive, where all their most precious belongings, the things too important for the trailer behind it, were stowed. She returned to her father and dutifully handed him the small toy.

"Welp," he said, the house has been owned by our family for two generations, and I won't sell it. I can't think for the life of my who'd want to buy it these days anyway, so no harm in us going back in for a minute."

He regarded his daughter's favorite keepsake critically for a moment before handing it back. In a strong voice, he said, "Well, bring it along and follow me." He stood and walked in to the house, without even giving Sarah a look to see if she was behind him. He knew that curiosity would make her follow.

His echoing footsteps in the empty living room took them both to the large bay window. He looked out at their yard, shadowed by towering mountains for a moment before he said; "Put your bauble on the windowsill, girl"

Sarah looked at him in confusion, and slowly tried as she was told. But she found herself unable to let it go.

"You're gonna have to leave it girl. I know you love it, but you'll have to leave it." Her father leaned down and took her chin again and stared at her. "This is the bit of mountain magic I told you I'd show you, sweetie. Now I know you love that foolish thing more than any one thing you own, Lord knows why, but you do. Now you leave that here, right here where you've had so much love in your life. But, if you wish with all your little heart, and you never stop wishing with all your heart, I promise you this. One day you'll come back for that little doll. You gonna wish it with all your heart?"

"Yes Daddy," came the church mouse like reply.

"Then you just leave it here."

She did.

REGARD

"And lo, the mountains were made straight, then the great distances were made short."

REGARD

Same doll, same room. The floor has lost its polish; the wallpaper hangs in uneven tatters. Time has moved on and treated the house unkindly. It is broad daylight. Thumps and voices pierce the stillness from another part of the house.

Nothing obvious happens for a while. In life, action sequences sometimes take forever to get to the right room.

Eventually though, the thumps get close enough, and the voices become audible as words.

"Remind me again why you insist on me coming with you for this?" says a woman's voice.

"Because, dear, I miss you terribly otherwise," responds a male voice, now closer.

"I get bored, you know."

"With a wit like me to entertain you, the devil you say," responds the man with feigned hurt.

Now the protagonists of this scene have entered the room. They are at the low end of middle age or the high end of simple adulthood; it could go either way, so let's say in their thirties somewhere. He is carrying tripod and other photography equipment. They are both dressed for hiking.

"You know, I don't get it some days. We live in the mountains, other photographers just shoot them."

"Hacks, my dear. Any idiot can make a pretty picture out of a pretty picture.

I hope the reader realizes there is no real animosity in this back and forth. It's more of a game to pass the time together. Most couples at some point fall in to some variation of a Grant and Hepburn repartee that is more for their own amusement than anything else. Variations on a theme, looking for a new zinger to add in to the skit.

122

He sets up his tripod and looks around.

"Oh will you look at that?" he exclaims softly.

"What?"

"In the windowsill"

"Oh, it's one of those old dolls. I forget what they're called."

"Yep. Yep, annnnnd I have my shot!"

The room falls quiet again, save for the twists and turns of the tripod, and the clicking of his camera.

"All right. I got what I wanted, lets head for home."

"Are you going to take the doll?" she asks.

He looks at it in its spot and considers. "Naw. It wouldn't seem right."

"How so?"

"I don't know. It's hard to explain. If it were a piece of furniture or something that looks like it still has life left in it I'll grab it. But sometimes something just looks like it belongs to these old houses."

She looks at the small and grimy doll for a minute. She picks it up, looks at it carefully, and then sets it back in its place. "Yeah, I think I see what you mean."

"Well c'mon. Let's head for home and tomorrow I'll owe you a waterfall or something nice and Thomas Kinkadeish. Deal?"

"And your committed to it now," she says happily.

With the same thumps and bumps and diminishing voices with which they came, they are gone again, and silence reigns again in this lost and lonely place.

REGARD

A woman is looking out a window at a green yard and a skipping boy. Mountains are in the background, and the boy is playing with a dog. His name is Richard. The woman remembers being told that in another place and time, it had seemed like a sad thing, but there is no sadness now. Just the joy of a boy and his dog playing.

Smiling contentedly, she leaves the window and goes to another room in the house. She reaches her arms around her husband from behind, seated in his chair reading a book. He says nothing but subtly leans in to her hug, not taking his eyes from his book.

"I wonder if the rest of the kids will get here soon?" she asks.

With a barely audible *harrumph* he closes his book, sighs, and says, "Hun, I've said it before, the kids are off making their own paradises. And isn't that enough for them? It is really fair to always ask them to come running to ours?"

She looks at the slightly hurt look on his face smiles and says, "Maybe not, sweetie, but you can't blame a mother for wanting all of her babies where she can keep an eye on them."

He relents and smiles. "I know, but we have each other and that's what matters most. The boy is outside being a fool with his dog, and you, are inside hugging me. Isn't that enough? Anywhere is fine, as long as it's with you," he grinned.

She remembers him saying it once before. She remembers it made her feel a great melancholy then, but now it fills her with happiness.

"Well," she says releasing him and standing up, "this particular anywhere has laundry on the line that has to come in." She turns to go outside.

She hums tunelessly, looking over the clothesline occasionally, checking on her son and his dog as she removes the clothes pins and fills the basket. They have now found their way in to the creek and are splashing along gaily. *Oh well, a mothers work knows no end, and laundry is why little boys and happy dogs exist.* Something every mother suspects deep inside.

She returns to the house and goes to the living room to fold the laundry, so as not to disturb her husband in the den. She sets the basket on the coffee table and starts on the pants first, smoothing out each pair crisply and neatly. Out of the corner of her eye, she sees something that makes her pause. She walks over to the windowsill and picks up the tiny kewpie doll sitting there. She smiles at it warmly.

"I told you I'd be back," she says, setting it back down in its place on the sill.

REGARD

Dirty moonlight through a windowpane, shines on a grimy little doll, the kind they used to give out at carnivals and fairs. But though the years have been kind to neither the window, the house, nor the doll, the smile shines on, fixed, and eternal.

Ed. note: This impressionistic piece leaves the reader with the feeling of having visited the nearly abandoned coalfield towns so common in the region. It's shifting person, tense, and perspective forces us to let go of convention and focus on images. Short story? Play? Vignette? Not easy to label, Country Road Reborn may be a ghost story, or a snippet of childhood memory, or something else entirely.

Hitting the Target
Samantha Mann

It was the day before deer season. Most of us had arrived the night before to the old farmhouse. The first ones there always had the luxury of turning on the electric, closing all the valves and starting the water pump, and cleaning up the mess left behind by mice, insects, and whatever else had been creeping through the house while the humans were away. Beds had to be made, refrigerator stocked, and a general cleaning done before unpacking all the guns, ammo, and hunting gear.

This was a routine for the family dating back to well before I was created. The farm existed within the West Virginia boundaries, but was one of those places where you couldn't get there from here. When I was young, the trip was often made in the back of a pickup truck among the hound dogs, gas cans, chain saws, and assorted snacks my mom packed for me but I was too car sick to eat. Back then, the ride took seven hours. Now, it only takes 4.5. It only took 50 years to straighten out some of those curves.

I could probably make the whole trip with my eyes shut. A routine I started before I was even finished baking, but it didn't stop there. Before I was old enough to hold a gun, I would participate with my family in the honored tradition of coon hunting. It was a special family indeed that waited till 10 pm, packed up the kids, hounds, and flashlights and set off to the woods. It was during one of these nighttime adventures that I learned about the value of experience and wisdom.

My grandfather had lost a leg to the railroad in his younger years. This didn't stop him from walking with his walking stick and wooden leg up and down the many hillsides chasing coonhounds. Since I was the youngest, I was also the one left without a reliable flashlight. On this particular night, my lack of proper lighting and a few stumbles through the dark woods had me following closely on the heels of my Pa. He led me across a fence and out into a cow pasture. When we were well out into the field, he stopped, turned his light off, and told me to stand there really still and quiet beside him. I would've asked why, but I remembered the somber instruction to remain quiet.

It was then that I noticed that the rest of the family were about 100 yards away and crossing the fence into the field, laughing and talking loudly, and causing their lights to weave and bob erratically. I didn't understand how this was any different than usual until they all started yelling, screaming, and trying to get back across the fence. It was a calamity like none you had ever seen. A half dozen people running all out and diving across a fence with each light bobbing in response and sounds I didn't know they could make. My grandfather never made a sound. He had rested his hand on top of the walking stick and was now resting his chin on the back of the hand. If I could've seen the details of his face through the darkness, I'm sure I would've seen a big grin on his face. Pa knew information that wasn't included in textbooks and couldn't be learned on city streets. He knew that cattle were known to stampede when they feel threatened. Erratic lights and laughter apparently were not polite behaviors for a cow pasture. The cattle were going to stamp out the offenders. Pa knew that by standing still in the dark, the cattle wouldn't see us as a threat and would avoid us with their attention drawn elsewhere. My family survived, mostly unscathed. Pa never said a word about any of it. But, what he taught me that night spoke volumes.

My study of my grandparents and parents became the study of the masters. They possessed in them the lessons and experiences of a whole culture. A culture of self-reliance and survival had created a curriculum that was not taught so much with words, but with acts. Things got used and reused. When buildings were torn down, even the nails were straightened for later use. Things that broke got fixed. Sometimes it was with duct tape or some homemade contraption, but it worked again and that was all that mattered. After I got older, visiting the family farm was like homecoming for a school I was proud to have graduated and a memorial for those who had passed on to other hunting grounds.

This day, the house had been resolved to our particular use and the weather was more like mid-summer than late fall. My brother had brought some friends to hunt with this year. They had arrived and were busy unpacking their arsenal on the front porch. I'm not sure why the harvest of maybe one little deer apiece was going to require assorted rifles and gear. But here they were, unpacking rifle after rifle and firing them one at a time at a piece of paper about 50 yards away and a metal target on the hillside about 150 yards away to make sure they were sighted. It was not new activity that we would sight in our guns before hunting, but usually this was done rather discretely and quickly. There was no need to waste ammunition after all.

The activity on the porch was busier than Wal-Mart on Christmas week. Guns were everywhere with each rifle having a whole bag full of gadgets, scopes, and slings. We could've given Cabalas a run for their money. I watched with some amusement wondering how much money had been spent and whether they were even going to take the meat home from their harvest. I figured that our small porch was probably holding $20,000 worth of materials and our total harvest might come to about $300 worth of venison. Don't get me wrong. I enjoy guns too. But what do guns have to do with hunting?

The valley rang with the fire of each round. The echoes across the mountains would repeat it back. It was loud and the gunfire repeated continuously for at least a half hour. I figured that every deer in the valley had headed out for new country after all the racket. I wondered how this practice fire might affect the enemy during the war. Either they would tremble at the noise and the amount of firepower demonstrated, or they would be laughing to themselves that we would run out of ammunition before the battle even got started.

As I made one of my trips across the porch and into the house carrying cleaning supplies, one of the fellas who was amazed that a woman was even there to hunt asked whether I had sighted in my gun.

I said, "No, my gun is usually always ready to go."

"Well, wouldn't you like the reassurance that it is still sighted in? When's the last time you sighted it?"

"My gun hasn't changed in two years. I sighted it back then and have shot it since. It still shot straight when I used it last year."

I then received an encouragement to shoot it and a condescending sounding short story on how his buddy missed the big one because he hadn't checked his equipment. I shrugged my shoulders and told him that I would check it in a bit. I looked down at the cleaning supplies in my hands and told him I had priorities. I suppose I may have been a bit condescending as well. In my family, it was impolite to play when there was work being done.

After getting the house arranged to my satisfaction, and after becoming annoyed at the constant barrage of rifle barking, I donned my eye and ear protection, grabbed my rifle and a few rounds of ammo, and stepped out onto the porch. I asked politely if I could have a turn to which all the men cleared the way to the shooting bench. I promptly ignored them and stepped into the yard. I loaded my rifle with one round, put it to my shoulder as comfortably and automatically as putting on a shirt in the morning. I took aim at the metal target on the hill, and steadied my breath. Everything was familiar and automatic. Even my thoughts were predicted as I ran through my routine of securing my sight on the target and holding it there while my hands went through the motion of gripping and pulling the trigger. The gun jumped, the shot rang, and the familiar clang of a metal target spoke back.

I suppose there is some pride in a well-placed shot. There is great satisfaction in using a tool that performs so well. There is also a nice reminder that the universe is still operating as expected. I ejected the spent round from the rifle and lowered the gun. I truly enjoyed this rifle and was proud to have such a fine tool that my family would approve of. This was a tradition that anchored me to the earth and connected me to my ancestors and my loved ones who were no longer visible. Firing my rifle is akin to practicing my religion. I almost feel embarrassed to do it in front of others. As I turned around, I saw that none of the fellas on the front porch, with exception of my brother, knew what had just transpired.

I quietly slung my rifle and carried it back to the porch and started toward the door. One of the fellas was looking at me as if he had seen something he truly could not understand. The others were making themselves busy getting their next rifle prepared to fire. I glanced at my brother and he had a knowing half grin on his face.

"Aren't you going to shoot it again?" said the fella who had provided the lecture earlier.

"Why? It apparently shoots just fine."

I placed my rifle caringly back in the rack and made sure that my ammo was ready to grab the next morning on my way out the door. I made myself a sandwich and sat at old kitchen table with aluminum legs and the red, sparkly, linoleum top that was worn down to the sub board in all the familiar places. I ate my sandwich slowly and crunched on the chips while listening to the battle continue in the front yard. I wondered if maybe my family had been the only ones in the world who understood what hunting really meant. If we are the only ones left....what a shame.

Late Spring
Warren Reuschel

The upper field was high on a shoulder of the mountain, where the trees and stones had long since been carefully moved aside to make room for forage. A broken stone wall and a chicken coop marked the edges of the field like a small and forgotten fort. The hollow below was already nothing more than a deep shadow as the last few rays of evening light left the field. Nathaniel felt a slow, creeping cold moving up the slopes as he piled his last load of litter into his truck.

He pointed the old Ford onto the dirt switchbacks and his lips quivered. Not from fear, nor from the cold, but from age. This year marked sixty-eight seasons that he had outlasted the winter in his own place, and dug into the rich earth of spring. Cold, especially March cold, was something he had learned to simply look at, through his frosty breath, but never feel. Fear was something that had dwindled with practice and patience, as he had seen his hollow give rise to life and death with the same predictability of the seasons; a thunderstorm in February would bring a frost in May, and an unanswered hoot-owl would bring a death within three days.

He pulled off at his cabin and placed his pitchfork in the shed, grabbed an armload of hickory kindling, and went inside. Odessa was asleep in the bed beside the woodstove. He had moved the bed into the kitchen the day his son and daughter had brought her back from Roanoke.

"She's plumb eat up in her back and chest," he'd said to Mr. Bailey in October when they sat together to eat a squirrel breakfast. His lips quivered then, too, but Mr. Bailey said nothing. The bells on the church in the hollow rang nine o'clock, and they finished their squirrel in silence.

He leaned over Odessa's still body, and kissed her forehead. "Onions" he said, holding up a bunch of green onions. She nodded and motioned for them. He placed them in her shaking hand, and she felt the dark soil still hanging onto the roots, the thin skin of her own fingers translucent in the yellow light of the kitchen lamp. She fell asleep again.

Nathaniel emptied her leftover protein shake — only a few sips were missing — into the sink. He seared a piece of leftover salt pork in a cast-iron pot, and added the fresh October beans he had set to soak that morning. He changed Odessa's bedpan and wiped her forehead, and held her hands while the beans cooked. When the beans were ready, he set himself a place at the small table and ate his beans and onions. That night Nathaniel dreamed he was a young boy, hunting foxes on the ridge above Pinnacle Creek. His best hound had fallen into a slide along a highwall, and Nathaniel was alone at the edge of the slip calling for him. The rest of the hounds had crossed over Clark's Gap into Widemouth, and he was alone in the dark. He slid down an old poplar trunk until he was near the bottom, and felt his way through the dark towards the hound's whimpers. Greenbriers caught at his face and arms as he pushed along an overgrown bench, and he felt blood along his neck. He crawled for what seemed like hours with nothing to guide him but the faint sounds of his hound. His heart and lungs burned and he could feel cramps working their way to his core. The hound was closer, now, he felt his way to the slumped mine entrance, where the noises stopped. He felt in his pockets for a match to strike.

In a brief second, he saw a brilliant light throughout the mine entrance. Old timbers sagged under the weight of hard sandstone slabs, and crumbled brick canopy was scattered to either side. The hound was sitting in the center of the lit area, wagging his tail. A young girl emerged from the shadows — his first baby, Lila, whom he'd buried when she was 18 months old and dysentery had struck when the spring went dry. Beside her sat an old man Nathaniel had last seen when he was a foreman at Tolliver and the refuse at McComas had carried him down Crane Creek. The light flashed blue – shooting back into the tunnel, and Nathaniel saw row after row of people smiling and waving at him. Then there was a roar, and Nathaniel heard singing as his body was blasted from the entrance.

He awoke to a cold room without the sound of roosters. The old ones had been boiled down for dog food, which he fed to his beagles and feists before giving them to Charlie. A few of the hens were taken by coyotes, and the last three he had cooked for himself and Odessa during the winter when she could still eat dumplings. He had told Mr. Bailey at Christmas "That doctor in Princeton kept telling her it was just fractures in her back, the cancer hadn't been around for nearly ten years. I'm getting rid of all the dogs and chickens, don't know what I'm going to do, she's plumb ate up."

Odessa didn't stir as he lit the fire and made coffee. He boiled an egg and made toast, then went over to her bed. He pulled up his chair and held her hand, and wiped a tear from his eye. Her hand was cold, and he sat staring at the woodstove until morning had passed.
After the funeral no one saw him leave his cabin for weeks. His truck sat motionless and the upper field sprouted bluets and blackberry blossoms. A coyote gave birth beneath the empty chicken coop, and deep in the stone wall chipmunks and copperheads advanced and retreated. Mr. Bailey stopped on Wednesday mornings to check on him, and they would share coffee in silence. The cabin seemed cold, even in late May.

On the first Wednesday in June, Mr. Bailey stopped again. No one answered the door. The Ford was still sitting motionless. Mr. Bailey pushed the door open, to the smell of coffee and beans cooking. Up on the shoulder of the mountain he heard a hound baying up a rabbit. As he turned to leave, Nathaniel pulled up on his tractor.

"Morning!" said Mr. Bailey.

"Morning" said Nathaniel, "I just come back from Charlie's. Got me some chickens."

And his lips quivered.

Daddy's Hands
Linda Lester Tabor

It was a beautiful, crisp October afternoon. The sun shone brightly on the crimson and gold colored leaves. The air had just enough chill to remind me that summer had indeed bowed gracefully out of the picture to allow the next season to step forward.

That day stands out in my mind, for it was the day my eyes, and heart, witnessed my father's and my life, coming full circle. Until months later, I would not realize what solace that day would offer me.

Dad had been in the hospital again. It seemed the last few years of his life he spent as much time in that cold, sterile environment as he did in his own home.

As I pulled into the parking lot at the doctor's office for his follow up visit, I could see the weariness surrounding him, his tired, fragile, body sat quietly, dreading, the too familiar routine it must once again face.

Opening the car door, I took his hand and helped him out. We began our short walk to the entrance. His steps were painfully slow and his feet shuffled against the concrete walkway. I held his arm through mine to help steady his balance. "Don't let go, he said, my legs are weak and I may fall."

At that moment, it was no longer the fall of 1992; it was the summer of 1974. His words, the vessel that transported me back to another place and time. A place and time that had taken its place among other recollections that sat in the back row of my memory.

As I sat on the dock held up by the waters of the Greenbrier River, my heart raced, and the perspiration forming on my upper lip had nothing to do with the July warmth. Being around open water instilled within me a fear like no other. Four years prior, when I was nine years old, I watched in horror as my sister was pulled from the lake and laid on the beach. She had drowned. Her lifeless body was white/gray in color, her lips an angry blue tone. I remember little about the ride to the hospital. Sirens and flashing red lights filled my head.

Once at the hospital, I ran to the bathroom. I sat in a stall with the door closed and prayed to God that all of this was a dream, "God, I pleaded, let me wake up now, please make this a dream, please take it away." But, a dream it wasn't, and on that day, I lost not only my sister, but also a part of my childhood innocence.

Now, as I sat on the floating dock, watching the others swimming, and enjoying a reprieve from the scorching heat, all I could picture in my mind was that day several years before. I wanted so badly to join them, but the fright was just too gripping. Sensing that I was in need of attention, my dad swam over to the edge of the dock and asked me to come into the water. Shaking my head from side to side, I could not release the terror I felt at the thought of feeling that cool water encasing me. Touching my hand, my dad said to me, "It will be ok, I promise, just try one time, I will be right there with you."

His persuasiveness finally paid off, and I found myself slowly stepping down the ladder and into his awaiting arms. As I stood up, my feet felt as if they were lead; I couldn't move. Gently, he urged me to take another step. My legs were numb and I felt tears streaming down my face, but I so badly wanted to show my dad that I was strong and capable of doing what he asked. Still holding my arm through his, we began making our way to the shallows where I could sit down. I heard my voice saying, "Don't let go, Daddy, don't let go, my legs are weak and I may fall!" His reply, "I will never let go, I will hold on tight, and I will never leave you." True to his words, we made it to the rock bed and he stood there holding onto me until I was comfortable enough to allow his hand to go free.

The chilly air brought me back from the past as I heard Daddy say, "I am sorry to slow you down, I just can't move so fast these days." "Daddy, I replied, "It's just time, no need to hurry."

In a matter of minutes, I had seen two very separate lives merge into a full, round circle, time intertwining age, and youth. I loved and respected my father so very much that I would have gladly taken his place amidst the slow, laborious, failing of his body. I felt the warmth of his hand as it covered mine, and, although it didn't have the same strength, it held the same love as it did, so many years before, on that searing July day.

Daddy passed away two months later, in December. As I sat in his dimly lit hospital room, the snow lightly falling outside his window, one more time my hand covered his. Tears of grief flowed without restraint. He had been so many things to me in this life. My best friend, my fishing companion, my keeper of secrets, my protector. Looking down at his hand and mine, I was comforted by the words he spoke so many years before, "I will never let go and I will never leave you."

And he hasn't.

A father's promise will be kept even beyond this earthly realm. In moments when I feel myself struggling, feeling as if I may fall, feeling my legs grow weak, and, heavy from walking a path that is littered with obstacles, I sense the hands of love reach down to steady me.

My dad on one side, my heavenly Father on the other, and I am so grateful for the knowledge that I am never truly alone, and will, for all time, have those hands to lead, guide, and protect my every step. After all, that's what fathers do.

Memoir

Ed. note: There was not a memoir section included in the original *Not Taking A Fence* outline. Sam Interdonato submitted a home wake memory piece, and then sent the first of the following pieces as his 'short bio' for the Contributors section. He is obviously a man with a story to tell! That story, chronicling the experience of immigrants coming to Appalachia from Italy in the early twentieth century and working hard to give their children a better life, fits our theme of civilizing the mountains. It shows an example of the worth in retaining old country traditions even after those who carried them across the Atlantic are long gone. There was no editing for passive voice and other subjective style anomalies here, so the lyrical, oral-history voice comes through. Rosalie Ash's funny and heartwarming *Cooking Fried Chicken From Scratch* will resonate with Appalachian readers of my generation, and captures the spirit of a girl's wonder about the adult practice of cooking chicken, taught by a patient and loving grandmother, so well that it won an Honorable Mention in the West Virginia Writers Incorporated competition in 2010. Evelina J. Butcher's spare, yet elegant reflection on the land and its influence on her life and family is touching in quiet a way that speaks to the heart. Would it be so hard for you to write a similar record of your life's journey? And to help someone else, perhaps further along the road, to do the same?

A Grandson of Italy

Sam Interdonato:

My parents had their second child three years after their first son was born. Charles Samuel Interdonato was born at the old Raleigh General Hospital in Beckley, West Virginia on Tuesday, April 29. My friends know me as Sam. My parents were Charles (Charley) and Mary Fondale Interdonato My brother Pete was born first. We realized that he was often looked up to because he was the first grandchild in the Fondale family. He was doted on by our mom's dad and large family as well as dad's mother. My sister Elizabeth Ann, or Libby, was the youngest and she got special attention from my mom, who had pledged that she would use her electric Singer sewing machine to make my sister an endless wardrobe of beautiful dresses. Wearing uniforms and attending Catholic school saved mom from debt. They did enjoy purchasing fabric and notions for their sewing passion. She made most of her own clothes and she often made curtains and anything that might be needed to keep the house bright and colorful. My brother and I would often get a shirt.

All three of us grew up with my Sicilian/Italian/American heritage as a very big part of who we are. The City of Beckley, West Virginia became a home to many families from Italy and City Avenue and several surrounding streets extending into Mabscott and Beckley Junction became the city of Beckley's Little Italy. City Avenue boasted that we had at least ten Italian families. Most were Sicilian, but a few families were from the Calabria region. My parents were always ready for company. We can all recall long Sunday afternoon visits from friends on the street.

My mother Mary was one of ten children. Eight survived childhood. She became the oldest child when two sisters that preceded her died in infancy. We either visited with her many brothers and their families or visited the home place in our earlier years. My one aunt who lived in the Mabscott home place was often at our house on the weekends.

My mother had a very warm and teasing personality, very quiet way, and talent for cooking that always brought everyone to our house. My mother could create many delicious meals from nothing, it seemed. We often went through more than twenty-five pounds of flour a month. She would cook every meal from scratch. We knew nothing about readymade, or store bought. Italian Sicilian regional dishes were in abundance, but Christmas and holidays were even more special. For holidays it had to be homemade pastas and pastries to go with American traditional foods. These desserts, pies, cakes and breads of every description, were to fill our dining room table. Mom and Dad worked in a bakery in the neighborhood, starting in the 1930's. The right spices and herbs were part of these dishes, and cinnamon rolls were one of my favorites, but all of them were to delight our palates and there was an endless list of favorites that we would often enjoy.

We had chickens in the backyard; a plentiful supply of eggs had to be used for baking. Fresh chicken was an ax and a back yard barn away. No one could ever forget the smell of chickens that were beheaded and scalded to remove feathers, but the taste was out of heaven and mom always added her fresh grown basil and parsley for the best chicken in town. Mom was a natural with food. She grew several gardens and provided us with plenty of fresh vegetables. She would can tomatoes, green beans, pickles, and peppers, apples for pies, applesauce, pears, and grape juice. Her cooking skills earned her a job cooking in our Catholic school, which was in the neighborhood. She could cook all day and come home and continue planning for large meals with homemade breads and pasta, candy, pies and Italian fried bread that is better than any doughnut.

My dad worked in a machine shop and he also did janitorial work. His last job was clerking at a liquor store. Our house sat on several large, mostly level lots that my dad inherited from his family. It was the place where all neighborhood kids came to play. My parents never would run any kid off, even when they broke a window or shingle. Mom often times brought food out to us or invited our friends in for a pizza or sandwich or spaghetti.

My education was at St. Francis de Sales grade school, located a few blocks from our house. We were taught by the Sisters of St. Joseph and lay teachers through eighth grade. The discipline was strict and children were held accountable. Parents were very supportive and our Catholic faith was very much a part of the curriculum. We were in large classes of over forty and we often talked about how everyone cooperated because high standards were set. I was often shy and sickly, with three cases of pneumonia before I was out of the second grade. I now wonder if the allergic reaction was due to my dad's cigarette smoke.

I had to work hard to overcome my shyness. It really would not happen until I went to college. After St. Francis de Sales, it was time for public school, with one year spent in Jr. High for the ninth grade during the first year of school integration in Raleigh County. It was painful leaving a protective parochial school for public school, where we witnessed students fighting for the first time.

High school followed as my education continued at Woodrow Wilson High School for grades 10 through 12. Some of my favorite subjects were geography and history and English. My hopes seemed to focus often about a career in teaching history, but many times history classes would be endless busy work and questions at the end of a chapter section, vocabulary and glossary terms to look up. It was my desire to have discussions, and talk about history, and hear stories about historical figures. We had all heard stories at home about a few of the most colorful Italians in our neighborhood. There is no doubt that the stories became "enhanced" with each retelling.

My ninth grade civics teacher during that tough year had seemed to keep my interest. It seemed like teaching history and social studies would be my career path after doing well in his class. My education continued at Beckley College and my tuition was paid with money that I earned from working part time at the local A&P, or Great Atlantic & Pacific Tea Co. My job was to clean the meat department, wait on customers, prepare hamburger meat, slice deli meats, and wrap packages of ham, chicken and beef. I spent many hours scraping and cleaning power saws and workbenches.

My next college experience took me to Marshall University in Huntington, West Virginia. My goal was to continue my career choice and study history and prepare for a career in teaching history or social studies. It is known that college and university classes can be difficult, but the classes and my studies and this curriculum along with various psychology classes in the Marshall Teacher's College seemed to be the correct choice.

I feared homesickness at first, but determination and desire to enjoy the experience helped me adapt. Reading every assignment and arriving each day for all of my classes helped me achieve success. One of my favorite classes was Russian history. It was a required class that brought drama to life.

My goal all along was to work and graduate and find that ideal teaching job. Money was in short supply, but I was able to curb and control spending and wasting money. I became the cook for two roommates. We did very well with keeping costs down and eating affordable meals. We lucked out with a great apartment across the street from Old Main.

Applying for teaching jobs as I completed student teaching at Huntington East High School went well. Job interviews followed and then I received a letter that changed it all. The letter stated that substitute teachers were in demand. There was a phone number to call for South Point High School, just across the river in Ohio. I read that letter over the Thanksgiving break. The principal told to come to work as a substitute teacher immediately.

There were still two weeks before my completion from student teaching and my graduation date at Marshall University, December 12. The principal told me to come to South Point on Monday, December 15. My dream was achieved, making me the luckiest person in our student teaching seminar. My career began with a detour, with what became a two-week stint at the Jr. High next to the High School. This old building from the 1930's looked like a haunted fortress.

On my third day driving over Huntington's 17th Street Bridge, fog enveloped my car. There was not one bit of visibility. Fog was so thick that it blocked my view across the car hood. I made it to the school. My immediate question was the why did the smell of ammonia seem to be so overpowering, and the answer was a lesson on the plant that manufactured chemicals in this Ohio village and over in nearby Ashland, Kentucky. I soon lucked out again when I was told to report to work at the high school. A full time sub job for the remainder of that school year was offered to me. Two more years teaching followed at South Point, Ohio.

My real dream had often been to go back to Woodrow Wilson High School in my hometown of Beckley, West Virginia. My resume was sent out and an interview followed. Impatience and worry about my next move followed and it was decided to go and check out the prospects. Throwing a suit in the car and driving to Beckley on August 6, 1978 happened to be fate stepping in again. Hearing about the death of Pope Paul VI on the car radio that day sticks in my mind.

My sleeping was interrupted early on my first day back. The phone rang. My mother said that it was Mr. Ross Hutchens, Woodrow Wilson High School principal. Everyone had the most respect for Mr. Hutchens. He earned his great reputation for being honest, strict and upfront. He told me to come over to the school for an interview. It was the best decision to put that blue suit in the car before driving from Huntington to Beckley.

Upon hearing nothing about the job until the third week of August caused more concern. My mom's friend called to say that she had seen my name as being the newly hired history teacher. She worked at the school. The job of teaching history was now mine. It was a welcomed challenge, and it now all seems like a dream come true for sure. No looking back with any regrets.

Time passes by so fast. My career ran full circle and ended with my retiring with thirty–five years of experience teaching at Woodrow Wilson High School. My experience with a varied list of classes helped me enjoy my many tasks with all phases of history, economics, government, United States, World history, the Civil War, etc. My first love was teaching Advanced Placement European History and an A/P U.S. history course. I always enjoyed researching and searching for information. I often threw in social justice, geography, cultural and intellectual history and the arts and architecture for each era that I taught.

I felt like I was where I wanted to be. I often did Saturday detention, selling ball game tickets and chaperoning many trips to ball games, various attractions in Beckley, The Capitol in Charleston, New York etc. My biggest thrill was to help take students to Europe on several trips abroad. My favorite was Russia, and Egypt, but the very best travel experience was Italy. I did make it to Sicily. My lesson on immigration and citizenship enabled me to incorporate all of my experiences and stories about my grandparents' immigration into the United States in order to work in the West Virginia coal mines.

I can recall Mr. Hutchens asking me at the end of my first year if I would be interested in teaching summer school. I subbed that first summer. I would continue to teach multiple grades throughout all my remaining years as a summer school teacher at the school.

My interest in teacher rights and benefits enabled me to become active in the West Virginia Education Association and later I became a building representative helper and then building rep. I enjoyed helping teachers with contacts and visiting the WV Legislature as a lobbyist on school policies. Our Raleigh County reps enjoyed working closely with one another to achieve better benefits and help other teachers stay informed.

Upon completion of my thirty-eight years of teaching and fearing the unknown, I was led to a volunteer job where my love of history could continue. Staying involved and informed is part of any retirement.

One of my hobbies has been learning about the General Alfred Beckley family. Being a tour guide and telling about General Alfred Beckley and his family and their life at Wildwood, the Beckley family home, brings our local history alive. Meeting some of the living members and descendants of John James Beckley and his son General Alfred Beckley is a great source of stories and experiences about real people that we can incorporate and blend into the legends of national and local history.

Membership in the Raleigh County Historical Society promotes pride and informative tours of Wildwood and allows the love of Beckley and the history of the General Alfred Beckley family to continue. The Raleigh County retired school personnel group has been active in Raleigh County with retirees. We have been working to insure that we continue earning our benefits, insurance and retirement plans. Our members also try to keep other retirees knowledgeable about policies dealing with their interests about retirement.

My interests also include an active membership at St. Francis de Sales Catholic Parish in Beckley. Attending mass each week as well as other services is something that I love and look forward to. Helping out as an usher and helping distribute communion as a minister of the Eucharist is a great honor, which gives another dimension to attending church. My involvement in the parish has continued with my membership in the Knights of Columbus. The Knights of Columbus is a fraternal organization for Catholic men. Its founder was Fr. Michael J. McGivney. He had a vision, and he hoped to keep Catholic men involved in the Catholic Church when many of these men were often pressured to leave the church and even change their surnames because of social pressures to fit into American society. Many immigrants faced discrimination.

The Venerable Father Michael J. McGivney was an Irish-Catholic priest in New Haven, Connecticut. He gathered a group of men from St. Mary's parish for an organizational meeting on October 2, 1881 and the Order was incorporated under the laws of the U.S. state of Connecticut on March 29, 1882. Many of these men and their families had immigrated for work and a better chance to raise their families in a safe environment away from constant war and battles in Europe. He brought his male parishioners together in New Haven, Connecticut in St. Mary's Church for the purpose of creating a fraternal organization for men that had become part of the work force during America's industrial revolution. The Knights of Columbus organization became a reality on March 29, 1882. Today the Knights of Columbus is the world's largest Catholic fraternal service organization. It was named in honor of Christopher Columbus.

Today, there are more than 1.7 million K of C members in 14,000 councils, with nearly 200 councils on college campuses. Membership is limited to "practical Catholic" men aged 18 or older. Councils have been chartered in the United States, Canada, Mexico, the Caribbean, Central America, the Philippines, Guam, Saipan, Japan, Cuba, and most recently in Poland.

Our charitable activities encompass an almost infinite variety of local, national and international projects, from international charitable partnerships with Special Olympics, the Global Wheelchair Mission and Habitat for Humanity to our own Food for Families and Coats for Kids projects and other purely local charities. The opportunity to work together with fellow Knights and their families is virtually endless. My membership also extends with membership in the Fourth Degree Knights of Columbus, which is a patriotic order. The Fourth Degree is frequently regarded as an honorary title with its regalia of tuxedos, capes, chapeaux and swords, but should rather be thought of in terms of service to church and country, and the goals of the Fourth Degree may be summarized as the promotion of the ideals of Catholicism and Patriotism side by side. My duties also include me being the Color Commander of our local honor guard. We participate in many church related ceremonies and also participate in civic parades and ceremonies such as the Beckley Veterans Day parade.

Volunteering at the Raleigh County Veterans Museum in Beckley has been another job that is enjoyable since my retirement. This museum has given me another chance to help give history commentary on many of the people from Beckley and Southern Western Virginia and share stories about the many that answered the call and served in the United States armed forces. The museum includes thousands of items collected from various wars and far off conflicts in which our military branches have served our nation.

It is with a sad heart that we remember one of the reasons why the museum has done so well gathering and preserving not only artifacts but also the stories about military history and its impact on our tiny corner of West Virginia. Jim Toler passed away on February 15, 2016. It was a totally unexpected shock. Jim had such a strong feeling for keeping our military history from West Virginia alive. We will always be able to see and admire his replica of the Battleship U.S.S. West Virginia. His model took seventeen years to construct and it stands proudly and helps us recall the ship with its crew and the crucial role that it played at Pearl Harbor, with its witness to the Japanese surprise attack on December 7, 1941.

Some of my hobbies include gardening and growing as many garden varieties of tomatoes, peppers, greens, green beans, squash, cucumbers and various varieties of roses and annuals and perennials as well as flowering bushes. A few favorites include iris, peonies, tulips, daffodils and others from what I can recall my mother planting. Gardens do save money. It is nice to incorporate my garden vegetables into my love of cooking. The cooking experiences challenge us. My sister Libby and I work at keeping up food traditions, preparing foods associated with holidays like Christmas and Easter. We cook together each Sunday so that we can continue all of the memories of family times.

Plants can brighten any space and taking care of a wide variety of plants is enjoyable. I still enjoy keeping a tropical fish aquarium that also brightens interior spaces. My hobbies also include several book collections.

My travels broadened my interests in collecting items from places that I have visited. I like collecting ships, sail boats, flags from countries visited and eggs in various mediums. Seascapes, palm trees and the beauty of the ocean and sea prompted me to collect shells and coral. Another passion is photography as a way to preserve memories about my travels, Knights of Columbus activities, my garden as it grows and progresses each summer, and photos are taken of our many winter snow storms. I may want to document all the events that I am participating in because of my vast interests in history and the desire to preserve it. I only wish young people and others would appreciate history a little more.

Smashing Spiders
Evelina J. Butcher

Smashing spiders and starting fires, that's what first comes to mind when I think of what living in West Virginia has taught me. Yet, I know it means so much more.

I've been here for almost three years and have learned more than I believe I've ever learned about myself, life, and others.

I'm not accrediting West Virginia for all of this, it's just that there is something about its proud beauty that causes one to reflect and quietly listen to what God has been saying all along. Or at least for me, that is the case.

I've lived in many parts of this great country and found something special in every place I've been. Yet, the one thing I was always looking for, I've never found—and that was a place to call home. I know this life is only a small moment in God's perfect time, so I pray this is the place He allows me to remain until He brings me to Him.

My fondness for West Virginia goes deeper than its physical beauty. The people here will steal your heart. At first they may seem remote and hard to get to know, but that is so far from true. West Virginia folks, (and I mean that in the purest form, no fun intended; I don't know how else to sum up their gentle and loving nature) are a cautious people, with a tendency to hold back at first, and that I believe comes from their history of being used and misrepresented. So often people professing to be friends have cheated them, so they have become a little suspicious of newcomers. Yet, once they've accepted you, it's hard to ask for finer people to call friends and neighbors.

There is a freedom here that is not often found any more. It's as if the mountains and trees call for you to join them in their joy of just being, watching the grass grow here takes on a whole new meaning. One day, you look out the window and everything is bare and brown, the next day, green has exploded all over and a feeling of new life is everywhere.

That awakening of new life flows over into one's creative nature and inspires whatever talents you may possess. Or, at least giving the urge to create and express oneself, whether it be musically, artistically, or with words as I'm trying to do.

Talent of one sort or another is home bred here; it is as much a part of West Virginia as the mountains. I've become accustomed now to, whenever more than a handful of family gathers together, someone will pull out an instrument of some sort and start playing. The music is just as much a part of family dinner as the abundance of good food.

I've also learned to listen to stories with the anticipation of a punch line. When I first arrived here, I would listen as someone, perhaps my husband or his father, go into a tale of woe and mishap wide-eyed and open-mouthed, only to have the finale of the story be some West Virginia tall tale.

I have discovered much about myself here, some good and some bad. But the journey has been in beautiful surroundings, with the company of good friends. West Virginia is wild enough to teach you how to overcome fears and show you strengths you never knew you possessed.

I may be slightly prejudiced on the subject of West Virginia, since my husband, whom I love dearly, is so much a part of this place. I could never see him living anywhere else. He can, and does, spend hours wandering the woods, just enjoying the life around him. He's always in search of his favorite mushroom, or that elusive ten-point buck which

146

I, in my little city heart, still think is more beautiful in the woods than on someone's wall.

I would say the biggest change that has occurred to me here is becoming the mom of a beautiful little girl. She is a part of West Virginia, or, should I say, West Virginia is a part of her. Its mountains, trees and hollows are a part of her history and, hopefully, will be a part of her future.

This is the place her father was a boy; it's his to share with her, as are the stories of his youth. This place called West Virginia, the home where they were born, the home I have proudly chosen.

Cooking Fried Chicken From Scratch
Rosalie Ash

Some of the best and most cherished memories of my childhood were of the times I spent learning things from my Grandma. Sadie Crawford was a saintly woman of French and Irish heritage. She had eyes the shade of a clear blue sky. Streaks of silver ran through her short curly hair. Her round moon-shaped face stopped just above the extra chins below her face. She always wore cotton printed housedresses. She loved to joke and play tricks on all the kids. Grandma and Grandpa resided in a two-story home high on a hillside near Huntington, West Virginia. At the time, it was like living in the country.

Sunday dinner at Grandma Crawford's house meant fried chicken, mashed potatoes, chicken gravy, green beans, corn (on the cob if it was summer), coleslaw, and biscuits with lots of butter, which she actually churned. For dessert, she made apple or cherry pie, cobbler or chocolate cake.

Probably the most vivid memory of time spent with Grandma happened the day she decided to teach me the art of frying chicken from scratch. One Saturday when I was about 12 years old, Grandma gave me her "I'm about to have fun look," which usually meant a practical joke was in the works. She announced, "Sis, it's time you learned to fry a chicken from scratch." The only thing I knew about frying a chicken consisted of removing it from the icebox, dredging it in flour, and putting it in a skillet. I'd watched Grandma do that many times. Grandma told me, "Go inside and slip on some old clothes." Appropriately dressed in old, stained shorts and shirt, I stepped outside into the afternoon sunlight and heat. Now, we could get down to business.

From the small woodpile in the corner of the side yard, we gathered several pieces of dry wood and stacked them on a spot where Grandma often built fires. She added crumpled newspapers to the wood, struck a match, and lit the papers and wood. Grandma placed a large pot into the metal frame that held it above the fire. She then poured hot water into the vat. I kept wondering what all this had to do with frying chicken from scratch. I was about to find out, and it was not one of her practical jokes.

Grandma informed me our next order of business was to catch one of the hens that roamed freely in her large yard. Grandma looked me in the eye and told me, "You need to find one of the hens and catch her. It won't be easy, but I'll help you." Being a city girl, I didn't know the difference between a hen and a rooster. I answered with, "You're kidding, right!" She was absolutely serious. I'm standing there wondering out loud why she didn't just get a chicken out of the ice box. But, she asked me, "How do you think the chickens get into the ice box each week?" I never really thought about it because every Saturday evening there was a chicken in there. I started putting it all together and things became a little clearer, the fire, the pot of boiling water, and now chasing the chicken. She didn't give me enough time to consider the situation at length. It was time to chase the chickens.

Several chickens ran loose in the fenced yard. Flowers and bushes, including snowball bushes, hydrangeas, and roses (with thorns) filled the yard. Her yard was full of blooming bushes and flowers. The fragrances from the flowers floated through the air with the most fragrant, sweet smell imaginable. She grew her own ruby red tomatoes, sweet corn, pole beans and West Virginia white half-runners. She raised a lot of other vegetables but these are the ones I remember the most. Also, in the front yard, two cottonwood trees towered high above everything. A swing large enough for two adults or three kids

148

hung between the trees. I loved that swing. Sometimes, Grandma and I swung for what felt like hours. I listened while she grabbed my attention with her stories about her childhood and family. Other times, we sang songs. After dark, Grandma told me ghost stories, which she swore to be true.

Toward the back hillside, Grandpa had leveled off a space and poured a concrete patio on which a glider and several chairs sat. Up the hill several more trees grew, and the two-seat outhouse was on another level spot. At the very back of the yard, Grandpa and his sons had built a large storage shed, which stood on blocks.

Soon, she spied a big white hen and pointed her out to me. When I attempted to grab this feisty fowl, she headed for the snowball bushes. Try as I might I could not reach her. Grandma shook the bushes. Out the white bird ran. Boy, could she run. She kept running and squawking. I continued to run, reach, and fall down. I chased that bird all over the yard into the bushes, flowers, and vegetables, under chairs and under the storage building. She squawked the entire time like a fox might be chasing her. I saw the terror in her eyes. I believe she knew what her future held. After all, she had lost several fellow fowl over the past weeks. When I closed in on her, she looked straight at me, flapped her wings, and acted like she was ready to attack me. When the hen and I tired of the chase, Grandma quickly grabbed her. I was dirty, bruised and scratched. No fried chicken was worth this much trouble. Grandma found the humor in what had just transpired.

Hen in hand, Grandma explained how we needed to break the chicken's neck to kill it. My mouth must have dropped to the ground. I pleaded and begged, "Can't you just buy a chicken at the store?" Her answer was a simple statement, "No, they're too expensive." With that said, she grabbed the hen by the head, flicked her wrist and broke the poor bird's neck. The hen did not appear to be dead. She flipped, flopped and moved about wildly. Grandma grabbed a piece of twine and tied the hen's legs together. Next the scene became so gruesome, I turned away. She held the chicken down on an old tree stump and with a hatchet chopped off her head. She tied the bird upside down to the clothes' line, and the blood dripped from her body. For several more minutes the fowl flapped her wings and moved along the clothes' line. When she finally stopped moving and most of the blood had run out, Grandma removed her from the clothes' line. By now, I felt as if I might throw up. The bitter truth was out. My beloved Grandma killed in cold-blood and now I was an accessory.

Feeling nauseous and faint at the same time, I headed for my swing between the cottonwoods. I needed to digest and come to terms with what I had witnessed. I'm thinking, "Sadie Mae Crawford, murderer, killer, my grandmother." Grandma joined me. She placed her arm around me and in her most soothing grandmotherly voice, told me, "Sis, I'm so sorry this upset you, but this is how we must prepare a chicken so we can eat it." She informed me that when I grew up, I would prepare chickens the same way for my family. Fat chance that would happen. I did not possess her pioneer spirit. It just seemed barbaric to me. She kissed me on the cheek, took my hand and led me back to the chairs she had placed near the vat of boiling water. We returned to the task of preparing the chicken. She assured me the worst was over.

Next, Grandma removed the chicken from the clothes' line. She held it by the legs, which were still tied together, and dipped it in the boiling water several times. Satisfied the chicken was ready for plucking, Grandma showed me how to grab a feather between my forefinger and thumb and yank the feather from the chicken. She plucked one side and I the other side. The longer we plucked the feathers, the worse they smelled. Wet feathers stink almost as bad as a wet dog that's rolled in a little bit of everything nasty. With all the feathers plucked, Grandma lit a candle and held it to the few pin feathers left on the dead bird. Once all the pinfeathers had been singed, she laid the naked chicken on the table.

After experiencing my reaction to the first part of the preparation, Grandma decided she needed to make sure I was ready for the next steps. She explained, "We have to cut the chicken open and remove the insides. Are you going to be okay?" I replied with uncertainty, "I guess so." She proceeded to cut the chicken open and remove the innards. She disposed of these in the trashcan. Next, Grandma showed me how to remove the liver, heart and gizzard. She cut these from the chicken and put them aside in a large pan. She pointed out a strange looking bag, which contained egg yolks. Grandma explained, "This was the hen's egg bag and would have eventually become eggs for breakfast or baby chicks." She extinguished the fire and carried the chicken to the kitchen.

While Grandma thoroughly rinsed the chicken, she informed me, "There's a right way and a wrong way to cut up a chicken. I'll show you the right way." "Thank Heaven, the worst must be over," the thought raced through my head. She laid the chicken on a large cutting board, found her sharpest knife, and began dissecting the chicken. First, she gently pulled one leg toward her, located the joint where the thigh joined the back. With a quick motion, she pulled the chicken's leg down and loosened the joint. She then sliced through the joint with her knife. Next, she separated the thigh from the drumstick in much the same way. Repeating her method of loosening and cutting, she removed a wing and placed it in a pan of water along with the leg and thigh. She repeated this procedure on the other side of the hen. Cutting the chicken in half required breaking the ribs and cutting through them. She then cut the back in half. Now, she was ready to cut the breast piece that contained the "wishbone." With her well-trained fingers, she found the "wishbone" and cut that piece of chicken away. Anytime we had chicken, two of the children held the wishbone under the table and made a wish. Then, they pulled the bone until it broke. The child with the smaller bone got their wish and the other child would marry first. This always brought a few laughs around the table. Finally, she showed me the last step. She flipped the breast over and sliced through it.

Because the chicken was for Sunday dinner, she rinsed it and placed it in a bowl of cold salted water and placed it in the icebox.

After we cleaned up the mess in the front yard, Grandma asked "Would you like some cold lemonade?" Of course, I answered, "Yes." It felt like an eternity had passed, but only a couple of hours had gone by. Lemonade in hand, we headed for the swing. A wonderful, cool breeze whispered through the trees like thousands of butterflies fluttering their wings.

Sunday - finally! Grandma poured some flour into a dish, added salt and pepper and mixed thoroughly. She heated a huge iron skillet and dropped several spoons of lard into it. She dredged each piece of chicken, including the heart, liver, and gizzard with the flour and placed in them in the sizzling grease. She browned the chicken quickly on both sides, lowered the fire to simmer, and allowed the chicken to cook for about an hour. Meantime, she prepared the rest of the meal. When the chicken was ready, she placed it on a platter. She browned some flour in the skillet, seasoned it, and added some rich cream to thicken it. All that remained now was enjoying the dinner, which I had helped fix. The brutality of the preparation to cook fried chicken from scratch bothered me a lot, but the chicken tasted amazing.

I will always cherish that Saturday and Sunday when Grandma taught me how to really fix fried chicken from scratch. I also declared I'd buy my chicken from the grocery store when I grew up and cooked for my family.

The End

Big Deathly Things, Taught Little
Danny Kuhn

When studying history in both high school and college, I learned about the Whiskey Rebellion, Haymarket Riot, Triangle Shirtwaist Fire, and Johnstown Flood. All four were mentioned in text books. Events similar, or even larger in scope and consequence, occurred in the Appalachian coal fields of southern West Virginia, but are generally only taught in West Virginia history classes, or have a line or two in specific courses on the history of American labor.

In 1886 Chicago, someone threw a homemade bomb during a demonstration in support of workers striking for an eight-hour day. In the aftermath, authorities were pretty lavish with the number of people they arrested, tried, and hung.

In Johnstown, Henry Clay Frick, a Gilded Age industrialist of the second tier under Rockefeller, Morgan, and Carnegie, and his friends bought an unused reservoir above the town to build a lake for a Pennsylvania Allegheny Mountain resort, all for the pleasure of his fellow upper crust ilk. They called their playground the South Fork Fishing and Hunting Club. Frick wanted easy access to both sides of the manmade lake, so he had the existing dam lowered to allow a road to be built over it. A fish screen (which also trapped debris) was installed so the wee fishes wouldn't go downstream to just be caught by some working class stiff, and culverts were sold for scrap.

On May 31, 1889, the compromised dam gave way, and the South Fork of the Little Conemaugh River briefly became equal in flow to the Mississippi. Two thousand, two hundred and nine people died.

Frick and friends were not among the victims.

Though they lost their pleasure pond, they did not lose money to anyone downstream. You see, they had structured the finances of the Club to prevent personal liability. They declared the Club bankrupt, walked away financially intact, and the tragedy was declared an Act of God.

During the Triangle Shirtwaist Factory Fire of March 25, 1911, one-hundred forty-six garment workers, locked into their New York City building by bosses suspicious of breaks and theft, died a horrible death. Most were young immigrant women, many in their mid-teens.

Thankfully, public outrage over the tragedy led to reforms and eventually the Ladies' Garment Workers' Union was formed, and caught traction in fighting for better conditions.

On August 1, 1921, Matewan, West Virginia Police Chief Sid Hatfield and his friend Ed Chambers, along with their wives, traveled to Welch, West Virginia for a court appearance. In broad daylight, Hatfield and Chambers were murdered on the steps, in front of their wives and numerous witnesses. Due to the corporate oligarchy that served as West Virginia state government in the day, the Baldwin-Felts "detectives" who murdered them never paid for their crimes, at least in this world. I trust they will do so eternally in the next. In *Fresh History, Brewed Daily: Raleigh County (WV) People, Places, Happenings 1750 – Present* (Favoritetrainers.com Books available on Amazon), I tell the story of a friend of mine, a second-generation Italian from McDowell County, who was a teenager at the time and an eyewitness to the murders.

The miners had had enough. Thousands of them decided that dying for change was preferable to being murdered by company thugs or, as so many did daily, dying in the mine because safety precautions cut into profits. Ten thousand of them massed to march into Logan and Mingo to unionize the coalfields.

The United States government called out the Regular Army, including its toddler Air Corps, to fight the miners. An estimated one million rounds were fired over five days. Many of the miners had, just a few years before, fought for their country in the trenches of France.

But, when U. S. Army machine guns and artillery and bomb-dropping airplanes arrived, Mother Jones pled for "her boys" to give up the fight. In hindsight, it would have been a bloodbath. The fight was over until the Roosevelt administration instituted protections for unions and other labor laws.

Compare that to the much better known Whiskey Rebellion, one of the first domestic challenges of the new United States government, in 1794. Farmers resented a tax placed on spirits by the flat-broke feds, and mustered a local force to resist. That force was of five hundred men.

It wasn't just the coal companies that had a free hand with the land and the people. Union Carbide, one of the world's largest and most influential chemical companies, still has a presence in West Virginia's Kanawha River Valley, sometimes referred to as "Chemical Valley," today. The industry evolved from natural resources found there that were exploited long before European settlers ever gazed on the area: natural salt brine wells that had been used by the Native Americans, and were the primary industrial resource long before the rich coal fields were exported.

The processes at Union Carbide's Alloy plant were power intensive. The company's subsidiary, the New River Power Company, deduced it would be more cost effective to use the river to produce hydroelectricity instead of building a coal-burning plant. Its contractor, Rinehart and Dennis Incorporated, was commissioned to construct a three-mile tunnel to divert New River under Gauley Mountain. They built a dam just below Hawk's Nest to divert most of the river's flow into the new course, to the power plant.

Gauley Mountain is made of sandstone, laid down by ancient seas during the Pennsylvanian and Mississippian geologic periods, from 358 to 286 million years ago. The rock is dense and solid, containing primarily silica. The construction produced a fine dust that hung thickly in the air the workers breathed during the entire three-year construction period.

Today, American hard rock miners are often required to wear respirators to filter silica from the air they breathe. Those worn by coal miners are designed to filter both silica and coal dust. Similar devices were available in 1927, and worn by managers as they observed the workers' progress.

Those workers, of course, were not given respirators. Not long into the project, workers began to cough up blood and weaken. It wasn't much of a problem for the project, though, because the labor did not require much skill, and a seemingly endless supply of men, many African-Americans from the deep south fleeing abject poverty and racial terror, showed up for work.

We can't be sure how many men died as a result of silicosis, as the disease is called. About 3,000 worked on the project; perhaps more than 1,000 of them died as a result.

Think about that. Due to preventable corporate neglect, a up to a third of the workers on the project died. Why were there not riots and a national outcry?

Unlike the Triangle Shirtwaist fire and the Johnstown Flood, the Hawk's Nest victims died slowly, painfully, over time. There was no photo op of burnt or mangled bodies. And, at the time, the lives of African-American migrants dying in an Appalachian tunnel during the great bubble run-up to the Great Depression garnered little attention. It was not until years later, during the New Deal, that it garnered any significant government action.

There are two historical markers in the area today. The more easily accessible, and therefore most read, states:

HAWK'S NEST TUNNEL

Mouth of the great Hawks Nest Tunnel, three miles long, which diverts water of New River from its five-mile long gorge. The tunnel, a mile of which is through solid rock, and a 50-foot dam give waterfall of 160 feet for electric power.

A proud monument to an industrial achievement, don't you think?

With effort, you can find and read another marker:

Construction of nearby tunnel, diverting waters of New R. through Gauley Mt. for hydroelectric power, resulted in state's worst industrial disaster. Silica rock dust caused 109 admitted deaths in mostly black, migrant underground work force of 3,000. Congressional hearing placed toll at 476 for 1930 – 35. Tragedy brought recognition of acute silicosis as occupational lung disease and compensation legislation to protect workers.

Union Carbide. Wasn't that the same company that owned the pesticide plant in Bhopal, India? The one that sprung a leak and killed around four thousand people?

The one that produced the same chemical in the Kanawha Valley, and some of it escaped in 1985?

I would never try to minimize the importance of the Whiskey Rebellion, Haymarket Riot, Johnstown Flood, or Triangle Shirtwaist disaster. But, there are some close-to-home things that also need to be remembered, and taught.

Old Bony Has Gone Missing, and It's a Shame
Danny Kuhn

Crime is wrong. That's why it's crime. Things like child or elder abuse or theft from old people or doctors trading opiate prescriptions for sex really burn me, and I dealt with all of those in my twenty years with the Federal Court. While not a Federal crime, this is also really despicable:

In January 2016, Saprina Roark and her husband found that her ancestor's grave, that of 36th Confederate Infantry soldier Thomas Meadows, had been robbed. Part of the old Rebel's skull remained, but the rest of his bones were gone. The remote family cemetery in Princewick, West Virginia is seldom visited, so Saprina was unsure when the crime occurred. She and the Raleigh County deputy investigating the case both suspected the same motive: treasure hunters, hoping to find gold fillings and Confederate relics, saw Confederate Veteran on the tombstone, and helped themselves.

At least one right-wing, yellow journalism national periodical postulated the sacred Confederate grave was desecrated by flaming Bolshevik radicals intent on avenging modern racism by disturbing the rest of a Lost Cause supporter.

Bull. Someone probably wanted to buy meth and couldn't find a convenient 4-wheeler to steal, in my opinion.

Thomas Meadows, being a Meadows of course, was related to a big percentage of Raleigh Countians still upright today, including me. As they say, anyone studying genealogy in Raleigh County must come to the conclusion that Adam was a Lilly, and Eve was a Meadows.

Thomas Meadows was born on January 8, 1835, the son of Jeremiah Preston Meadows and Nancy Cadle Meadows, who married on March 17, 1826, in Giles County. Jeremiah Preston Meadows (1804 – 1859) was the son of Jeremiah Isaac Meadows (1764 – 1843). Jeremiah's other children included William Henry Harrison, Richard, Jeremiah II, Sarah Jane (married a Hylton), Nicholas, Isaac, Rufus, Malinda (married a Birchfield), Elijah, and James. Rufus Meadows, by the way, was the father of the first West Virginia governor to hail from Raleigh County, Clarence Meadows. Old Jeremiah Isaac Meadows, son of Josiah Francis and Mary Kesiah Bell Meadows, moved to New River onto the land eventually owned by William C. Richmond, an area that used to be known as "Briery Bottom." If you hike along the river at that point, you know the name makes sense, even today. It was owned by Isaac's brother-in-law, Peter Davis. He is buried in the Meadows/Cadle cemetery in Jumping Branch, with one of those wonderful hand-carved native sandstone rock markers.

Nancy Cadle Meadows, the mother of our stolen soldier, was born in 1806, the daughter of Thomas and Nancy Holt Cadle. The tombstone states, "Dedicated by Thomas Meadows to his Father & Mother." Our Rebel honored his parents.

Thomas married Nancy Agnes Walker (1840 – 1911), the daughter of Charles and Rachel Karnes Walker. This union was on January 28, 1866, and is recorded in Wyoming County, but most likely took place in the Slab Fork District, which was part of Wyoming until it was ceded to Raleigh in the 1870s. Charles Walker (1813 – 1895) had the honor of being mentioned in the diary of a Union soldier attached to the occupying force in Raleigh Courthouse during the Civil War. The Yankee officer listed Charles Walker among the seven people who *"agree to remain peaceably at home if we will not molest them."*

The soldier doing that writing was Rutherford B. Hayes, later to become the 19th President of the United States.

Thomas and Nancy owned a considerable swath of property in the Gulf area. I only find one child who survived to adulthood, Martha Jane, (1868 – 1953). She married John Harvey Tolley (1857 – 1937) and had a fairly large family. They are buried in the Riverview Cemetery in Summers County. More on the John Harvey Tolley family a bit later.

The 36th Virginia Infantry, first known as the 2nd Kanawha Infantry Regiment, was organized early in the War. It was assigned to General Floyd's Brigade, and fought at Cross Lanes and Carnifax Ferry in what is now West Virginia and later moved on to Tennessee before returning east to the Shenandoah Valley, attached to General Early. It fought its last battle at Waynesboro. Field officers included Colonel John McCausland and Thomas Smith, son of Confederate general and wartime Virginia governor William Smith. He was in Company C 2nd, nicknamed the Raleigh Rangers, organized on June 3, 1861, originally for a one-year enlistment. It was later reorganized as Company E. It is said our Thomas was wounded twice during his service.

The roster ('muster roll') of the Raleigh Rangers includes many surnames still found in the area today. The officers included Benjamin Linkous (Captain), Christopher Roles, Enfield Thomason, and George Tucker, Lieutenants; Robert Witten, surgeon; William Beckley, Eldridge Henderson, Lewis Cook, and Charles Fipps, Sergeants; and Matthew Ellison, John Crawford, John Jones, and Abdel McClure, Corporals.

The homes of the soldiers could well be told by the names of the various companies in the 36th Virginia, such as the Logan County Wildcats (Company B 1st), Boone Rangers (Company B 2nd), Chapmanville Riflemen (Company C 1st), and the Fairview Guards (company K).

Back to John Harvey Tolley, husband of Thomas and Nancy Meadows' daughter Martha Jane. John Harvey Tolley's obituary offers something seldom seen in those days: reference to an airplane pilot in the family.

Hinton, July 13. – Funeral services were held Tuesday afternoon at Pence Springs for James Harvey Tolley, 80-year-old prominent resident of that place, who died in the Hinton hospital of an intestinal ailment that was aggravated by a fall. Rev. Lynn C. Dickerson, pastor of the Greenbrier Baptist Church, of Alderson, officiated and burial was in the Riverview cemetery near Alderson. Mr. Tolley was the father of James Tolley, well-known Pence Springs air pilot. He was born in 1857 near Mountain Lake in Chiles County, Virginia, the son of Preston Tolley and Katherine Snidow Tolley.

In 1883, he married Miss Martha Jane Meadows, of Raleigh County, and moved to Pence Springs in 1904 to engage in farming and fruit growing. He was widely acquainted in the surrounding communities.

He is survived by his wife; a sister, Mrs. Lanza Davis, of Pamplin, VA.; two brothers, Thomas Tolley of Montgomery and Callyhill Tolley, of Pamplin; and these children:

Mrs. J. W. Ward, of Beckley; Mrs. D. L. Fleshman, of Basset, Va.; Mrs. Rodney Foster, of Pence Springs; Mrs. John Keller, of Alderson; and James Tolley, of Pence Springs.

Nine grandchildren survive, among them being Miss Ruth Tolley, of Pence Springs, and Miss Margaret Ward, of Beckley.

The pilot James Tolley mentioned above, born in 1900, operated the Hinton-Alderson airport beginning in the early 1930s. He was a commercial flight examiner with the FAA, operated charter flights, and operated a flight school. During World War II, he operated a war training program in Princeton, connected to Concord's Civilian Pilot Training program.

Civil War veterans were starting to become scarce when Thomas Meadows died in 1921, though the last fully-verified veteran, Union drummer boy Albert Woolson from Minnesota, died in 1956. Veteran reunions, common through World War I, started to dwindle.

Grave robbing, unfortunately, has a long history. Many of the burial tombs in Egypt that were discovered in the late 19th and early 20th century, and even today, had already been plundered, sometimes before the birth of Christ. That is why the best hidden, hence the hardest to find even now, are the most productive from both a treasure and archeological knowledge viewpoint. You see, just like in Princewick, grave robbers aren't usually very careful about not destroying anything else that stands between them and gold. For several centuries, it was the corpse itself that was the target, because the robust trade in human specimens for medical school dissection, which was often illegal and conducted in secret, was so lucrative.

Thomas Meadows was buried in a glass-topped coffin, fashionable at the time. I hope the publicity around this crime does not spur copycats. And, I hope that, by the time anyone reads this, the people who disturbed his remains are residing at Mt. Olive, and Thomas has been reburied, with respect.

The above being said with all sincerity, I am almost reluctant to mention that, like so many people, Thomas Meadows was commonly known by his nickname. History, just like the present, is, well, what it is. In life, the prosperous old soldier was known by family and friends as "Bony."

Ed. note: Fresh History, Brewed Daily: Raleigh County (WV) People, Places, Happenings 1750 – Present (Danny Kuhn, 2015, Favoritetrainers.com Books, 340 pp., available on Amazon) contains many articles in this style. This piece, inspired by a recent news article, is part of an anticipated Volume II. This is, unfortunately, not the only grave robbing incident from modern Raleigh County, West Virginia. In 1981, a young science teacher at Liberty High School decided it would be a fun idea to run a contest among his students, with extra credit being the prize for bringing in various types of bones. Different points were assigned to monkey, buffalo, elk, and other remains. Allegedly, "Human" was marked with a double asterisk referring students to a written warning, reading "At your own risk. We are not responsible." The teacher was eventually charged with Contribution to the Delinquency of a Minor after the grave of Icy Snuffer in Bolt was opened down to the six-foot level. The dig was discovered when only a few inches remained before it would have encountered Ms. Snuffer's remains.

Home Wakes: Editor's Introduction
Danny Kuhn

In our not too distant past, death and its immediate aftermath was much more familiar to us than it is today. Though it still comes to us all, the actual act and its necessary preparations have been removed from our homes and relegated to hospitals and funeral parlors.

Our ancestors would be puzzled by our current practices. Why would we choose to remove our relatives from the place and people they loved, in their final hours before being committed to the earth? Why would we not spend that time with them, all night, instead of sending them to a cold and formal commercial establishment to be left alone except for a couple of hours?

The origin of the word *wake* is sometimes misinterpreted. I have heard more than one person suggest it came from the days before medical technology could always discern between death and a coma, resulting in the occasional event of a corpse literally waking up. Indeed, the fear of premature burial was rampant in the 1700s, all the way up to around World War I. Among George Washington's last words were his instructions to "not let my body be put into the vault in less than three days after I am dead." Even one of the bravest men in history, with his dying breath, wanted to ensure against being interred prematurely.

One entrepreneur even devised a system that placed a wire in the deceased hand that led up through the ground to a bell mounted on a shaft at the grave's surface. Should the decedent awaken and pull the wire, the bell would ring and a watchman, hired specifically for the purpose, would hastily dig up the coffin. The practice gives us terms still common in or work-a-day world. He's working the graveyard shift. She's a dead ringer.

Or, at least, so they say.

In reality, the term *wake* is from the Old English *wacian*, to be awake and keeping watch. It was associated with a prayer vigil during the feast day for local parishes, a time when the community gathered to pray, rest, and socialize; in other words, to reinforce communal ties.

The evolution of burial practices in Appalachia followed technology. Embalming is ancient, of course, as the Egyptian mummies attest. But the event that made it commonplace in America was the Civil War. Families understandably wanted their fallen fathers, sons, husbands and brothers brought home for burial, and embalming was the only thing that made that possible. At the time, formal, government-orchestrated burial of fallen soldiers was a hit-or-miss proposition. Armies fought and quickly moved on, either in chase or flight, with the grisly task of burying the quickly putrefying corpses left to the local farmers. Except, that is, for fallen officers. One's status, just as today, made a difference.

When embalming was done in the late eighteenth century, it was often at the deceased's home. The embalmer would bring all the necessary tools and chemicals, and sometimes even enlist the aid of the family members. In those days before one-stop-shopping for all things funeral, the wooden coffin was purchased separately from a carpenter, or, if someone had the skills, home made. One Peter Coleman, who was widowed for many years after his death, "broke up housekeeping" and lived with various members of his family for almost twenty years before he was laid to rest in Paw Paw, along the Virginia-Kentucky border. Evidently a considerate man who wanted to save his children trouble, his homemade coffin accompanied him on each visit.

In the late 1800s and early 1900s, more affluent families opted for glass-topped coffins, which afforded easy view of the deceased while keeping away flies and other insects. The superstition of keeping cats out of the house during wakes probably had its origin in a grisly reality.

The stories below, actual memories of home wakes, give us a good idea of the process. In later times, the body was taken to the embalmer and returned to the home, and then taken to the church for the funeral. As coffins became more elaborate, houses could not always accommodate them, and having to take windows out of their frames to pass the coffin through was common.

So the family would be relieved of the task to preparing food for themselves and mourners, visitors brought it themselves. Some went home in the evening, but true friends stayed the night, "sitting up with the dead." There had to be sufficient coffee and food to last the duration. There were even specific recipes for the occasion, and "Funeral cake" can still be found at family reunions (even those in which everyone is still upright) and church homecomings today. One variation:

Ingredients
- 1 cup (2 sticks) butter, at room temperature, plus butter for greasing the pan
- 2 and 2/3 cups all-purpose flour, plus flour for dusting the pan
- 1 tablespoon baking powder
- 1 teaspoon salt
- 2 cups sugar
- 4 large eggs
- 1 cup milk
- 1 ½ teaspoons vanilla extract
- Nutritional Information

Preparation
1. Preheat oven to 400 degrees. Butter and flour a 9-inch spring form pan.
2. Sift together the flour, baking powder and salt. Set aside.
3. In a bowl cream together the butter and sugar. Add the eggs one at a time and beat thoroughly. Fold in the flour mixture alternately with the milk. Stir in vanilla.
4. Pour into prepared pan and bake for 10 minutes. Reduce oven temperature to 325 degrees and bake 60 to 70 minutes longer, until the cake is brown and a cake tester comes out clean. Cool on a rack for 10 minutes, then unmold and continue cooling.

My own father did not want a wake, and they were becoming less common by then. He, as many, opted for an hour of "viewing" at the funeral home before the funeral. "They're just a big family reunion," he said. He was, of course, right. But that's the point. Those home wakes of the past were, as well. Yes, there were tears and sobs. There were also stories and food and conjectures about the eternal whereabouts of the decedent and sneaking out onto the porch by young mourners of opposite genders and opportunities to catch up and be with one another during lives that afforded precious little time to do any of those things.

Depending on the family, the 'sneaking out' may also have been done by older males, who would come back in a bit more conversant, if less coordinated.

The practice of friends and family members "saying a few words" at, or just before, the funeral seems to be catching on in Appalachia, though it was previously left strictly to the clergymen. I think it may be a way to try to regain something that has been lost when wakes moved out of the home: a sense of community and participation. For some reason, many funerals in times past were a two-man job, with obituaries saying the rites would be officiated by Rev. Eugene Ledbetter, assisted by Rev. Leroy Fife.

I was born in 1959, and have never experienced a home wake. I was a bit surprised to find, in these stories, that they were evidently more common into the 1970s than I imagined. Our family always had wakes at the funeral home, but that's what they were called, and I was unfamiliar with the term "viewing" into my thirties. I just hadn't encountered it. That led to an awkward exchange with a coworker once, when she said she was going to a viewing that evening. I knew she had been looking at houses and assumed she was meeting a real estate agent to view a new one, leading to my expressing hope that she enjoy it, and would find just the right one.

I have told my family that, when the time comes, we should revive the home wake practice. Cremation alleviates the need to reinforce the floor and take the windows out of their frames. And, as to adults having the need to 'sneak out', I've got you covered. You see, despite my German surname, I'm Irish. And if young couples need to go out for a little air? Feel free, with my blessing. Just don't let a cat in…and I can't even tell you why.

A Young Life Lost
Lois Abshire

I lived near Fayetteville W. Va. in the year 1943. My two brothers had gone rabbit hunting one cold fall morning, hoping to get some meat for dinner. They split up and went different ways in case the rabbit changed directions.

A shot rang out and one brother shouted, "Did you get him?" The reply came back, "No, I shot myself!"

His brother carried him out of the woods on his back, but he died from his wounds a few hours later at the hospital. The safety on the gun had failed. My brother, Boyd Jennings Underwood, was only 16 years old.

Boyd's body was taken to the funeral home in Fayetteville and then brought home in a hearse and placed in the parlor/bedroom. I remember my mother checking his clothing and putting socks on his bare feet to keep him warm. Friends and neighbors came with homemade pies and cakes and other food to feed the crowds of people that filled the small four-room house and spilled out into the yard. People came and went, and some stayed all night.

His body stayed at our home two days, and the funeral service was held in the front yard. Then he was taken by hearse to be buried in the family cemetery, high on that mountaintop.

My dad was working in the coal mines at Kaymoor, West Virginia when this happened. He worked in the coal mines about thirty years, worked as a meat cutter at one time, and retired after many years from the metallurgical plant at Alloy, West Virginia. He lived to 101 years old.

My mother, like every other women I knew, had a full time job at home. Monday was wash day, using two #2 round tubs with a standing hand cranked winger between them. I remember when she got her first Maytag. A neighbor could not make the payments so the salesman made a deal.

166

Tuesday was ironing day, using an iron heated on a coal burning stove. In the summer time, it was canning the food we grew for the winter...that kitchen sure did get hot! My mother was diagnosed with rheumatoid arthritis in her thirties, and it was sometimes so severe that she was confined to bed and we would have a "hired girl" come live-in to help out. Of course, we kids had our jobs as well. We had chickens, cows, and hogs that had to be cared for.

The fear of losing another child would come to this family about three years later, when the writer of this was struck by lightning while taking clothes off the clothesline, a single bolt on a sunny day, I'm told. But, that's another story!

Memories are fresh as yesterday for this brother, who would soon have been ninety years old as I write this. God bless you! This was my first wake.

Ed. note: According to official records, Boyd Jennings Underwood was born in Mossy, West Virginia on May 26, 1927. The hunting accident occurred on November 27, 1943, and he died the following day at the Oak Hill hospital. He was the son of Everett. A. and Annie Wilson Underwood. The couple had married on November 17, 1924, in Fayetteville, by J. W. Legg. Everett was the son of Virgil Everett Underwood, born in Floyd County, Virginia in 1872, the son of Warren and Mary Eddings Underwood.

Annie was the daughter of Harry L. and Matilda Wilson. Harry was born in 1868, died in April 1941, and had been a foreman for the WPA. His parents were William and Bettie Price Wilson, married in 1865 by Martin Bibb. Young Boyd Jennings was laid to rest in the Wilson family cemetery, which is also the final repose site of Anderson Wilson, who served in the Confederate Army, 10th Company, 142nd Virginia Militia. He had been arrested by Union soldiers on November 12, 1861.

The Gentleman of the Crowd

Eva Smith-Carroll

Leonard Haliburton Vest, 79, died on March 20, 1960, in his home on White Oak Mountain, Raleigh County, W.Va. He was a retired coal miner and farmer and the father of eight children. Leonard and wife Emma Stella lived "out the path" from their daughter and son-in-law Golda and Earl Smith.

Around dusk, Leonard became ill and said to his wife, "Stella, get me in the bed." She got him in bed and then went outside to beat on an old washtub that was hanging on the porch wall. We didn't have telephones, and that was the quickest way to summon my parents.

Arrangements were by the Ronald Meadows Funeral Parlor in Hinton. The body was brought home. Grandpa had told his family he didn't want a wake at the funeral home, where people would get cookie crumbs in his coffin. Light refreshments were, no doubt, also served at home. But maybe his reasoning was mourners would be more careful in the family home and confine their eating to the kitchen.

In 1992, Nina Vest Worley wrote about her father, "[When] the old men came to the casket when he was demised – I heard one say to another, 'He was always the gentleman of the crowd.' Knowing my daddy, I knew it was true."

Grandpa was buried up on the hill in the Smith Cemetery with his grandsons Billy Lee Smith and Bobby Lee Smith, who had died in childhood. It was bitter cold and snowy. His grandson Lee Hinte remembers the coffin being brought up the steep incline to the cemetery on a sled pulled by a bulldozer. The men – family members and neighbors – had dug the grave in the frozen ground with some help from gasoline to melt the snow and a light dynamite charge.

Ed. note: Leonard Haliburton Vest was born on November 27, 1880. He married Clara Alice Plumley on March 5, 1901. After Clara's death, Leonard married Emma Stella Gadd on June 11, 1907. Leonard was the son of Columbus "Lum" Washington Vest and Malinda Jane Cochran Vest, a daughter of Charles and Ruth Radford Cochran.

Lum's father, Jackson Vest (1832 – 1917), was a Confederate soldier, Company B, 23rd Virginia Infantry. He was married to Nancy Lilly Vest, a daughter of Robert "Bearwallow Bob" Lilly.

Death Bridges the Centuries
George Cole

I have been to many wakes, all before I turned the age of 13. I did not know what they were called, though.

On September 14, 1946, my brother, Kenneth L. Cole, was shot in Cool Ridge, West Virginia. He was one month away from being 18, and I was eight months past my eleventh birthday.

Kenneth was working on Saturday, September 14, 1946, with our father. Kenneth was an apprentice carpenter. Kenneth, along with LeRoy Meadows, Harry and Fred Goldie, set off for the two mile walk to see his girlfriend.

The family was at Sunday school on Sunday morning (September 15). Someone came into the church and went to the front, where my parents sat. I cannot recall who that person was. My mom and dad left hurriedly. I did not know what had happened until after church let out, about noon.

I was at a loss. He was one of my older brothers. He was my idol and I held him to the highest regard. It hurt so much and left me not only sad, but also empty. Since we shared the same bed, who was going to keep my back and feet warm on those cold winter nights, as we had no heat in the upstairs bedrooms? I hurt even more when I found out that he was shot and dragged, like a dead horse to its grave. They dragged his body to a rail fence corner to hide the body. I wished the one that shot him to burn in Hell!

The wake was held at our home in Cool Ridge. My mother and father removed all of the furniture from their bedroom and that is where they had the casket placed.

When Calfee Funeral Home brought his body home, they set up curtains all around the bedroom. Then the casket was surrounded by a lot of flowers.

People started to arrive during the late afternoon. Some brought food; they would stay awhile and then would leave. At that time, we had just gotten electricity and we didn't have a refrigerator, so everything had to be eaten up rather quickly because all the food could not fit inside the icebox.

Others came and stayed the night. Some people who came for the wake were: Frank and John Lane, John Goldie, Dean Pack, and Les Harvey. They were all there at 2:00 in the morning, when I woke up. I can remember going into the room several times to view my brother's body. My brother and I were very close. To this day, I can still picture him lying in his casket.

The day of the funeral, the funeral home came and took his body to Glade Creek Missionary Baptist Church. It was about 200 feet from our house.

There were so many people at his funeral. The church was full and a lot stood outside. Many of them were from Shady Spring High School. His body was then moved to the Kirk Family Cemetery in Cool Ridge.

I do not know the name of the shooter. All I know is that he ran the only beer joint the Cool Ridge.

Another death came on January 14, 1948. One day before his 88th birthday, my grandfather, George Washington Cole, passed away. He was laid out in my parents' bedroom, and was buried on my thirteenth birthday. People came and went throughout the day, bringing food. Some stayed awhile and a few stayed the night. I remembered getting up around 3:00 in the morning and people were still there. I helped dig his grave up on the hill in one of our family cemeteries, with about eighteen inches of snow on the ground. They took his casket up the hill on a sled pulled by two horses, and everyone followed on foot.

Everyone who was at my brother's wake was also at my Grandfather's wake, and all people mentioned above are now deceased.

Ed note: These memories from Mr. Cole clearly show the great societal and demographic transition of the mid-twentieth century. As a youth, he lost his older brother, an apprentice carpenter full of promise who might otherwise still be living today, to a tragic homicide. Just over a year later, Mr. Cole attended the wake of his grandfather, who was born before the outbreak of the Civil War. George Washington Cole, born January 15, 1860 in Ashe County, North Carolina, was married to Judith Pack Cole, and was the son of Joshua Joseph and Malinda Sluder, who married in Ashe County on February 10, 1858. Joshua Joseph Cole was a Confederate soldier who was wounded at the Battle of Missionary Ridge in November 1863. Taken as a POW, he later died of his wounds and is buried in the prison cemetery in Blue Island, Illinois.

The Midwife's Tales
Judy Foster Gerow:

My grandmother was the local midwife and "dressed and laid out" the local deceased. Bessie Leona Fitzwater Foster, born July 31, 1882, died on May 31,1970. I am Judy Foster Gerow, born 1950, not dead yet!

My grandmother was a great storyteller. She told me that she would wash and dress the deceased bodies for her neighbors in the now defunct town of Wyndal, in Fayette County, West Virginia. One story I remember is how they covered one particular deceased man with a white sheet and were having an all night wake. They were sitting around having conversation as to whether the man's soul was saved and so on, when the sheet started moving. It scared the jeebeejies out of them and some vacated the premises, not necessarily by the door. My grandmother was made of sterner stuff and got up and lifted the cover to find the man's pet cat stretched out on top of him.

This happened in the early 1900s. Almost all the Wyndal inhabitants moved across the river to Belva when the state road went through in early the 1900s. That's where I was born. I remember going to wakes when I was small, before 1960. Most of them were friends and relatives. Poor people couldn't afford funeral homes.

Ed note: Records indicate that Bessie L. Fitzwater married Van Buren Foster on December 2, 1901, in Fayette County, West Virginia. Van Buren was the son of Jonathan Nelson "Johnson" and Emily J. Foster, and Bessie was the daughter of Jacob Portsman and Edna Nichols Fitzwater, married in Nicholas County in 1866. Van Buren is listed as being a carpenter.

Jonathan Nelson "Johnson" Foster lived a long life, having been born in Humphreys, West Virginia on May 8, 1948, and died in Belva, West Virginia on June 2, 1950. He worked on a steamship for the U. S. government during the Civil War. In 1947, the Nicholas County Chronicle offered a brief biography of what was probably the county's oldest citizen at the time:

When Johnson Foster and his wife, Mary Hughes Foster, rejoiced at the birth of a son on May 8, 1848, they could hardly hope for that son to still remain a mentally active citizen of that locality ninety-nine years afterward, yet such is the case with Jonathan Foster of Belva, W.Va. Jonathan Foster whose picture appears above was born about two miles up Gauley River from Gauley Bridge. After he grew to manhood, he married Emily Cobb. They established their home a few miles farther up and across Gauley River not far below Belva. Uncle "Johnty" as he is familiarly known does not leave his room of recent years but his mind is remarkably good for his age and he takes quite an interest in things around him. He enjoys the company of his friends and is especially pleased when young people call to see him. His granddaughter, Ruby Stone and his two daughters, son-in-law Lud Dial and in fact all of the family seen to take especial good care of uncle Johnty Foster. So far as the writer knows he is the oldest citizen of Nicholas County, though there may be older ones.

The community of Wyndal, like so many southern West Virginia coal towns, is now essentially abandoned. Located on the Gauley River, it was part of the great Kanawha Coalfields. Its United States Post Office closed in 1930. At one time, it was not accessible by any road, but only by the New York Central Railroad and swinging bridges across the river, like the nearby coal camps of Vanetta and Gamoca.

When Death Came to Little Italy
Sam Interdonato

My first experience with death came when I was six years old. On a warm June 6th, around four o'clock, my mother called the three of us to come over to our house from the neighbor's yard. Her voice seemed urgent. She had been told that her dad had passed away. We then had at least four of the older Italian ladies sitting in our living room as they offered comforting words to us. I still recall my sister and I asked if our nono's (translation = grandfather) death was a result of his being in the barn with his cow. My grandfather, Phillip Fondale (Faudale) Sr. had been born in Fieumedinisi, a village in the Province of Messina, Sicily on August 4, 1887. He had immigrated to the United States because of some recruiting for men to mine coal in Southern West Virginia. He and many of his friends and acquaintances followed their dream. They finally settled in Mabscott, West Virginia.

My grandfather, or nonno, was found by several neighbor kids. He had been watching his cow graze. He was lying on the ground. We drove up to the home place on that Friday evening. My mom and her sister were very upset. I can still recall a man telling the family that they would move some of the furniture around like they had done before. My grandmother had died in the house on Victory in Europe (V-E) Day, May 7, 1945.

My godmother and godfather came from the same Sicilian heritage; my nonno had bought my godfather Sam his first coat when he came to the United States at age sixteen. My godmother stepped in to take care of us and our two cousins from Cincinnati, Ohio.

Uncle John was married to my godmother's sister. She had a huge house with two kitchens, a bathroom, antechamber and large yard. She was happy taking care of all of us and her three children. She entertained us with games of cards. The War game distracted us. She cooked and got us dressed. My godfather Sam drove all of us to Mabscott Hill to our first visitation at my Mom's family home on Sunday afternoon. I can recall many 1950's model cars parked along the unpaved road.

My mom was seated in the kitchen. We went into the living room, and my godmother had told us that our nonno would look like he was sleeping. I can recall the purple color of the velvet on the kneeler in front of a bronze colored casket. His mustache had been trimmed down. I can still see his rosary in his hands. The large oval picture of my maternal great-grandparents was not hanging in its usual place on the wall, but instead there were many vases of flowers and some sprays of flowers hanging on the walls. The blue couch had also been removed from the room. I recall that my dad had tears in his eyes. We then ended up outside, seated on folding chairs along the cement porch and side walk along one of his gardens, bordered by a very long grape vine harbor.

My mother and her family shielded us by not taking us to the funeral at the Catholic Church. I can recall waking up and calling out for my mom in the first bedroom at the top of the stairs at my godmothers house. and she came into the room to comfort me.

It was again a warm summer day five years later when our Italian neighbor Luigi died. He died following surgery after a long illness. I walked to the back door of the house across the street from ours with Tony, a neighbor boy. We were greeted by Josie and Nancy, Luigi's daughters. The family had gathered and was eating in the kitchen. I cannot recall that we ate during our visit, but we went into the living room, where his body was laid out in front of a large window. Pots of flowers lined the way into their living room.

Our deceased neighbor, who was a large man with aloud voice, seemed much smaller than how I had remembered him, laying in the casket. The dog next door was named Blackie. She had puppies under our chicken barn on the morning of Luigi's funeral.

As an altar boy at St. Francis de Sales, I was often called on to serve at funerals, since our home was one street down from the church. I attended many funerals, but I did not attend another wake until I was in high school. My first wake at a funeral home was for a grade school classmate. He died about two weeks before we graduated from high school.

174

My mother was very protective, and she never forced us to attend wakes or funerals. My mom and dad attended every funeral of every Italian from our circle of friends. They were as dependable as the postal system, no matter what the weather was like. My dad always offered rides to the older Italian neighbors in our neighborhood. As the custom of attending wakes in the family home gave way to visitations at funeral homes, they were still very faithful to attend and give support to grieving families.

As an adult, I have tried to be respectful and attend wakes and funerals of the many relatives and acquaintances that I have known from church and work. I can recall my dad talking to Carmilo, an Italian man that we knew. We were at a funeral home that has served most of the Italian and Catholic families in town. Carmilo told my dad that "most of the Italians end up here at this funeral home." Ironically, Carmilo himself passed away within about three months of making this remark to my dad.

The Young and the Old
Phyllis Kuhn

When I was sixteen years old, we lived on a farm in Monroe County, West Virginia. All of the little ones who went to school got the measles. I had a baby sister about six months old, and she got sick. They called the doctor; that was back when they came to your house. It was a woman doctor, and her last name was Smith.

The baby cried day and night, and I took turns with my mom rocking her. One morning, she got worse and the doctor came back, but the baby passed away while she was there. It was only then that she broke out with the measles.

That was in 1947. In those days, they let the body lay at the house. The neighbors came and stayed all night and did the cooking.

My Grandpa and Grandma Bennett, on my daddy's side, were laid out at their son's house at Gatewood, in Fayette County. The neighbors would come and sit up all night and cook for their family, too.

Ed. note: The Calvin and Roxie Sheaves Bennett family moved from Gatewood to Ballard, Monroe County, during World War II. Of the sixteen children born to the couple, thirteen survived to adulthood. Calvin was the grandson of Andrew Bennett, a member of the 30th Battalion Virginia Sharpshooters, CSA. Andrew is buried at New Salem Church in Raleigh County, WV. Roxie Sheaves Bennett was the granddaughter of Joseph A. Sheaves, Co. A, 26th Battalion, Virginia Infantry, CSA. He is buried at the abandoned coal camp of United in Kanawha County, WV.

A Young Korean War Hero Comes Home

Loretta Cooper Lilly:

When my cousin was killed in action in the Korean War, my mother, Opal Wood Cooper, had just given birth to my brother Curtis. She couldn't go to my cousin's wake. I was listening to a conversation between her and my sister, Louise. I remember my mother telling my sister she wanted her to go to my aunt Stella Cooper Farley's house in Odd, West Virginia with my father, Edward Cooper. My sister was to wash dishes and serve food. I didn't understand why she needed to wash dishes and serve food because someone had died, because I didn't realize they sat up all night.

My father later told us about the wake. A military person stood guard at the casket. My aunt wanted to make sure it was her son in the casket, so she chose my father and one other person to look inside and make sure it was him. The casket was so heavy that they had to reinforce the floor of the house.

My cousin was John Earl Farley, born November 19, 1929, and died November 5, 1952. His parents were Luther and Stella Cooper Farley.

Ed. note: John Earl Farley was a Private First Class in the 31st Inf. Reg, 7th Infantry Division, killed in action at age 22. He is buried in the Cooper Family Cemetery in Odd, West Virginia. His parents, Luther and Stella Pearl Cooper Farley, were married on December 26, 1914 in Odd, West Virginia, by Rev. McKinney. Stella was the daughter of

176

Andrew Anson and Annie Meadows Cooper. Luther was the son of John Albert and Emma Jane Lilly Farley. He lost an eye in an explosion at the Leckie Fire Creek Coal Company mine in Fireco.

A Winter Home-Going
Loretta Lusk

It was January 1, 1953, the same day that Hank Williams died. Although I was just six years old, I vividly remember the details about my Grandma Lilly's death, especially her wake. The day prior, Grandma was very sick and had insisted on eating a big bowl of "Leather Britches" for supper. Daddy suspected the illness was a problem with her gallbladder. My older brother found her partially out of her bed and unresponsive. After waking my parents and alerting them to the situation, the task at hand was to figure out how to get a doctor there.

The nearest doctor was in Coal City. We lived up Woodpeck Hollow in Sullivan of Raleigh County, West Virginia. So far we had a harsh winter and still a foot of snow lay on the ground, with single digit temperatures. We didn't have a phone, so my brothers set out walking down the railroad to my Aunt Lola's house, where they were able to call Doc Riley. Doc said he would get there as quickly as he could. With road conditions so treacherous, the doctor had to leave his car at Sullivan Camp and make the rest of the journey on foot. He confirmed what Daddy had been thinking since the day before. Her gall bladder had ruptured. Doc Riley tenderly took my dad's hand saying, "Aubrey, I'm sorry. Your mother is gone." He then proceeded to write some things down on paper: date, time, probable cause of death, etc.

After making his way back down the railroad to Aunt Lola's and breaking the news to her that her mother had died, he called the funeral home and requested that they come to get Grandma's body.

The undertakers had to park across the railroad, cross the creek, and then climb up a steep path carrying a stretcher. The worst part was that they had to take the same route back...carrying Grandma. With the help of my brothers and older cousins, the undertakers managed to get across the ice-covered rocks, logs and partially frozen waters of Piney

Creek. The boys still talk about that memorable night and their fears of slipping and dropping Grandma into the creek!

I began hearing lots of talk and chatter about something called a "wake." I asked myself, "Why would the words death and wake be used together?" I was already confused by the things I had seen and heard, and I didn't know what to expect next. I certainly never imagined that it would include sitting up all night looking at Grandma's body there in a casket.

The wake was to be at Aunt Lola's house. The undertakers weren't about to try to take Grandma back up Woodpeck Hollow. The hearse, donned with chains, arrived at my aunt's house. Cousins, grandsons, and funeral home attendants proceeded to carry the coffin to the house. When the men discovered that the coffin wouldn't fit through the door, they set it down on the porch and huddled in conversation. They then gathered up tools to dismantle the living room window. They removed it completely (and I mean every splinter) so that the opening would be large enough to squeeze the coffin through. I can still picture the scene of Grandma's casket being passed from the porch through the window to the room where the all night vigil would take place.

The undertakers placed the casket in just the right place in the room and opened the lid. They appeared to be doing something to Grandma. I guess they were making sure she looked okay. A tall, dim pink light was placed at both ends of the casket. The room began to fill with family and friends who had traveled to say their good-byes and pay their respects. The kitchen and dining room were filled with people partaking of the abundance of food brought in by friends and neighbors. The folks in the "Wake Room" were seated, speaking to one another in hushed tones. I eventually wandered into another room and found a bed where I could get warm and I soon drifted off to sleep.

I awoke at dawn the next day, and went to the kitchen looking for my parents. My mom took me by the hand and told me that I needed to go and look at Grandma and tell her goodbye. It was still dark and gloomy in the wake room, though daylight was beginning to peep through the windows. A mesh drape was hanging over one end of the casket, but I took a quick glance at Grandma. I guess I had heard too many fabricated stories about "sitting up with the dead." At mid morning, the coffin bearing Grandma's body was taken out of the house the same way it was brought in. The funeral was held at Coal City Community Church, and Grandma was laid to rest in the cemetery behind the church.

A lot had transpired over those few days, maybe too much for this little six year old girl to take in. It's been over sixty years now and other members of her family, even her children, have passed on and are buried alongside her.

Several decades have gone by, and the traditions and customs of all night wakes have changed quite a bit. Today it is the practice to have a "viewing" which lasts two or three hours the evening before the funeral. And so it is with many practices from over a century ago, we still remember how it was back then.

I will never forget the memories of Grandma's all night wake and her winter home-going.

Rest in peace, Grandma.

Ed note: According to records in the West Virginia Archives, Mary Susan Cox Lilly was born in Hinton, West Virginia on February 18, 1875, the daughter of James Lewis and Katherine Meadows Cox. They were married on July 22, 1873, in Summers County by Reverend Rufus Pack. Katherine was from the Francis Meadows/Kesiah Bell Meadows line.

Grandpa Samp's Send-off
Von Moye

My Grandpa, Sampson Lee Lilly, passed in 1974. His wake was at his home just a 1/4 mile from the Lilly Reunion Monument on Ellison Ridge Road, along the Raleigh/Mercer County West Virginia border. "Samp" Lilly owned and operated sawmills supplying lumber for building and timbers for the mines. Samp was the first to have a Model A Ford in that area, with the hand crank on the front. He used it to deliver mail in the area. He was a teacher and a big supporter of the Lilly reunions, which bordered his land in Flat Top.

Being a Lilly, he had hundreds attend his wake. I remember it was midday when visitors started arriving and the many, many cars that lined both sides of the gravel highway for about a mile. When I realized just how many friends and relatives were attending, I got my Super 8 movie camera and captured this on 8mm film, along with taking a still picture with a still camera. Many of the folks brought food for the family, as this was common during a death so the family could have more time to talk with friends and not have to concern themselves with cooking big meals. Many would shake hands, hug and share stories of how they knew Samp, and it just seemed as a big reunion itself. This lasted all day and way into the night. Being 56 years old, I can still remember this and the huge amount of people that attended.

Ed. note: The Lilly family of southern West Virginia has the honor of being listed in the Guinness Book of World Records as having the world's largest family reunion. Doing family history in the area, it sometimes appears that "Adam was a Lilly and Eve was a Meadows." Sampson Lee Lilly was born on August 3, 1894, making him a nineteenth century personage. His parents were Benjamin Byrd Lilly (1872 – 1955) and Celia Jane Lilly Lilly (1877 – 1935). Benjamin's father was Thomas Edmund Lilly (1833 – 1914), a Confederate soldier who, according to family legend, was being held as a Union prisoner when his first wife, Mary Akers, died. Home wakes were becoming rare by the time "Samp" passed away in 1974, when his grandson Von, then age fifteen, wielded his Super 8 camera that day. Von is a lifelong talented musician and has known many of the country music legends in Nashville.

PawPaw's Last Smile
Janet Ransom

My grandfather, William Carl Ransom, died in early January 1970. The snow was knee deep (to me, being probably twelve inches or so) and my Dad carried us down to the house from the chicken house lane, two at a time. My Grandfather had a huge industrial chicken house, as he raised pullets for market, and the lane was just above their house in Shady Spring, West Virginia. I was eleven years old at the time of his death.

The wake was held in their home and my grandfather was in the "front bedroom" off the living room, in his casket. The house was filled with people. My Dad came from a family of ten children, but at the time of my Grandfather's death, only eight were living. But, as you can imagine, with spouses and children, the house was packed even before church people and others came to pay their respects.

Two things stand out about this wake, the only one I went to in a private home. First, the snow was deep and it was SO cold. For the second, let's visit a bit. We were told to go in the bedroom where the casket was and give PawPaw a goodbye kiss. So we went in there and did so. My sister Joyce came back out and told my Dad, "Pawpaw smiled at me when I kissed him," and that she was very happy about that. At once, the Funeral Director went in the bedroom and shut the door to glue my Grandfather's lips back together, since he wasn't supposed to be smiling.

Ed note: William Carl Ransom was the son of James Henry and Nancy Ellen Lilly Ransom, who were married by W. L. "Elder" Simmons on March 11, 1896 in the bride's home. James worked for the WPA, and died on July 3, 1940, as a result of injuries received in an automobile accident. His father, Isaac Ransom, was born in North Carolina, and his mother, Elizabeth Meadows, in West Virginia.

From the *Beckley Post-Herald,* January 15, 1970:

William Ransom Dies; Rites Set 'Funeral services for William Carl Ransom, 73, of Shady Spring will be at 2 p.m. Friday at the Shady Spring Community Church with the Rev. L. A. Garten in charge, assisted by the Rev. Gene Hall and the Rev. Oscar Lilly. Burial will follow in Blue Ridge Memorial Gardens at Prosperity. He died at 1:40 a.m. Wednesday in a local hospital following a long illness. Born Jan. 3, 1897, the son of the late Mr. and Mrs. James H. Ransom, he was a member of the Community Church at Shady Spring and a veteran of World War I. Survivors include his wife, Rhoda Ransom; four sons. James C. and Huey, both of Parma, Ohio, Duren, Titusville, Fla., and George Clacy, Shady Spring; four daughters, Mrs. William (Bernice) Lowery and Miss Wanda Ransom both of Shady Spring, Mrs. U. S. (Ellen) Lilly, Mechanicsville, Va.. and Mrs. Daphne (Lois) Redden. Brunswick, Ohio; two brothers, Walter Woodrow and Kenneth, both of Blue Jay; four sisters, Mrs. R, C. (Agatha) Carter, Mrs. Fred (Sylvia) Carter, and Mrs. Basil (Ocie) Lilly, all of Blue Jay, and Mrs. Sudie Lynch of Glen Morgan. The body was taken from the Webb and Neal Funeral Home to the residence at 3 p.m.

Contributor Biographies

Rosalie Ash, a resident of Lesage, West Virginia, attended Marshall University. After high school, she worked as a continuity writer for WSAZ-TV. She then worked for twenty-seven years for law firms, followed by twenty years for the United States Probation Office. Her love of writing continued as she wrote freelance for the *Cabell Record*. She entered the annual West Virginia Writers' contests, and won awards for her efforts, including first, second, third, and honorable mentions. One story was published in the group's anthology, *And Now the Magpie*. She also had short articles published in *Woman's World Magazine*. Her entry in the Most Like Erma Bombeck category won an honorable mention. In 2010, Rosalie published her first book *We Fought Back*. Her second book, *Al Qaeda Pivot*, a collaboration with two other authors, is scheduled for release by early summer 2016.

Jonetta Bennett's ancestors were early settlers in southern West Virginia, but her genealogical research reveals they once lived in Salem, Massachusetts. That discovery made understanding her family much easier. She now splits her time on a north-south gradient. Her short story, *Arsh Mountain*, is published in *Mountain Mysts: Myths and Fantasies of the Appalachians* (Headline Books, 2015).

Matthew Burns was born and raised in Beckley, West Virginia and now lives in Princeton, where he works as a pizza delivery driver and operates an electronics business. As a single father trying to get by in rural West Virginia, he finds much solace in writing. For Matthew, as it is for many others, writing is a necessary means of expression while dealing with day-to-day triumphs and failures. His work reflects his underlying philosophy: *On this new frontier, as we all seek meaning and try to remain useful and relevant, it is important to remember that life is only as complicated as you make it.*

Evelina J. Butcher is an Appalachian transplant. She has lived throughout the United States, and traveled abroad, but is most proud of her self-transplanted West Virginia roots. She has lived there for nineteen years with her two teenage children, husband, and their many cats and dogs. She is a freshman at Marshall University and has been writing poetry and short stories since she was a child. Travel and reading are her passions.

George Cole was born in 1935 at home in Cool Ridge, Raleigh County, West Virginia. He was the sixth of nine children, and attended a one room school, K-8, and then to Shady Spring High School for 3 1/2 years. In 1954, he moved to Chicago, Illinois, and joined the Air Force in 1956. He spent time on Eniwetok Island during the Atomic Bomb testing, and then a year in Korea. George retired from General Motors after 30 years of service in Kalamazoo, Michigan

Justin Di Cristofaro states, "There is a veil between being completely lost and willfully indifferent. That is the narrow space in which I live." Painted in black, and dripping in silver, he sits at his vanity. This is where the candles are lit, and exorcisms of the chemical are written. He swirls a glass of chardonnay and becomes a ghost in his own mind.

W. M. D. was born and raised in southern West Virginia, living in Logan, Wyoming and Raleigh Counties. W. M. D. loved the mountains and the peaceful setting. Graduating from WVU in Industrial Engineering and working in and with various industries, his vocation took him from NC, MD, and DC but his heart was always in West Virginia. Inspired by West Virginia's hard working people, nature, culture and his brother's writing, he has provided a sampling of his writing.

Judy Foster Gerow hails from Fayette County, West Virginia and is a graduate of Gauley Bridge High School. She is retired from her career as a manager for People's Drug/CVS.

Renee Haddix is a writer who was born and raised in Philippi, West Virginia, a small, old-fashioned town nestled between the mountains. Reading and writing have always been her passion, and she remembers listening to old tales spun at the knees of her Appalachian family when she was a child. She believes those stories sparked an imagination that still serves her. She has two wonderful teenagers, and a hard working coal miner husband. They love animals, and have a house full of them to show it. They also love to travel and try to live their lives to the fullest every day, with a Live, Laugh, Love philosophy.

184

Sam Interdonato is a native of Beckley, West Virginia, graduate of Marshall University, and thirty-eight year veteran history and social studies teacher. He volunteers at Wildwood House and Veterans Museums in Beckley, and maintains many of the traditions brought to Appalachia by his Italian ancestors.

Sabrina Jones is an Appalachian-born writer and English teacher. She has spent half of her life in the Marshall University community, first as a B.A. and M.A. student and now as an instructor. She enjoys the stereotypical English teacher hobbies of reading and writing, especially YA fiction, Appalachian literature, and anything dealing with the American dream. She lives with her husband, son, and cat in Hurricane, West Virginia.

As a professional hydrologist, **Lee Keene** views fiction as a welcome break from the technical manuals that usually fill his day. His yet-untitled new collection of short works, in the experimental form he calls "flash flood fiction," is pending release. He was a contributor to *Mountain Mysts: Myths and Fantasies of the Appalachians* (Headline Books, 2015).

Marion R. Kee was born in 1956 in Charleston, WV and raised on its West Side hill. She treasures her time spent on her grandparents' working hill farm in Roane County, WV, and began creating stories and poems in childhood. Marion sent herself to Ohio University in Appalachian Southeast Ohio, studying everything she could get her hands on. She worked in computer science for many years. Marion holds degrees from Ohio and from Carnegie Mellon. Her poetry and creative nonfiction have earned multiple awards in the West Virginia Writers, Inc. annual contests. She lives with her husband in the Pacific Northwest and visits Appalachia often. Her poem *"On Hearing Bill Withers in the Ninth Grade"* appeared in the WV anthology *Fed From the Blade*, edited by Cat Pleska and Michael Knost. A lifelong musician, Marion sings alto and plays the upright bass—and yes, she plays bluegrass.

A former social worker, high school science teacher, and Federal Probation Officer, **Danny Kuhn** is the author of *Fezziwig: A Life* (2015) and *Thoreau's Wound: A Novel of Ireland and America* (coming December 2016), both released by Knox Robinson Publishing, London and New York, and *Fresh History, Brewed Daily: Raleigh County (WV) People, Places, Happenings 1750 – Present.* Along with P. Ray Lewis, he is an editor of *Mountain Mysts: Myths and Fantasies of the Appalachians* (2015, Headline Books, Terra Alta, West Virginia.) All are available on Amazon.com.

Phyllis Kuhn was born in Fayette County, West Virginia, but moved to a farm in Monroe County with her parents and their large family during World War II. She enjoys travel and writing about her life.

Eunice Lewis spent much of her childhood in Blue Jay, West Virginia, where she was the daughter of a company store manager. She was an amateur historian and genealogist and phenomenal bluegrass and rock-a-billy musician able to play nearly any musical instrument she attempted. Eunice devoted much of her adult life to the flea market circle, where she made many lifelong friends. Eunice was known for her collection of antiques and her appreciation for coins. Before settling down at 4-H Lake Road in Daniels, West Virginia, with her husband of over 40 years, Mack Lewis, she and her cousin played music together for a number of years on the local circuit. She was the mother of four children, and grandmother of writer/editor P. Ray Lewis.

Loretta Cooper Lilly is the daughter of Edward Cooper and Opal Wood Cooper. She is married to James Lilly and has two sons, Jimmy and Wayne, and grandchildren. She was born in the coal mining town of Stephenson, Wyoming County, West Virginia, on Barkers Ridge, at 4:00 A.M. on Easter morning. She lived in and out of coal mining towns until moving onto Raleigh Seven Road, Beaver WV. She is number six of thirteen children, and a retired Cosmetologist. "I always seem to be in the middle of everything for some reason!" she says. Loretta and James are active as tireless volunteers in the Lilly Family Reunion Association.

Paul Lubaczewski is a native of Philadelphia, Pennsylvania and has lived all over the country as a musician in the punk band The Repressed. He finally moved to West Virginia over a decade ago with his wife and son because "it's beautiful and people have manners." He's an avid caver and hiker, so West Virginia had some appeal. He has written as a rock critic for *Spark Plug Magazine* and his fiction has appeared in various magazines. His photography can be seen in numerous websites, often of his adopted hometown of Bramwell WV. His caving articles have appeared in the *NSS News* and *Speleo-Digest* as well.

Loretta Lusk was born and raised in Raleigh County, West Virginia. Her dad was a coal miner, and they always lived in the coal camp closest to where he worked. She is one of twelve children, all of whom attended elementary school in whatever little mining town they happened to live in that school year. She attended Sophia and Woodrow Wilson High Schools. She is the mother of four children and twelve grand children. She enjoys attending the annual Lilly Reunion, where she serves on the Genealogy Committee and the Board of Directors. Researching family history and genealogy is her passion.

Samantha Mann was born in West Virginia and grew up in the outdoors knee deep in creeks, making mud pies, with a rifle in her hand, on a boat, on horseback, or on skis. She has remained in West Virginia and lives with her awesome husband and four legged friends. She knew when she learned what the word meant, by the age of 14, that she wanted to be a psychologist, so that's what she did. She has had the benefit of a wonderful family and great mentors. She is a breast cancer survivor and is an advocate and volunteer for the cure. When she's not at work, she's spending time with family and friends shooting, hunting, Irish Road Bowling, and watching movies. Occasionally, she might write a little just for fun.

Sarah McHatton was born and raised at the base of the Great Smokies in the small town of Cosby, Tennessee. The ancient footpaths paved the love she developed for her heritage, the land, the view, and the community in which she grew up. Married to a Navy man, McHatton was able to see many parts of the world before resettling in the shadows of the Smokies. Earning a Bachelor's degree in English, she began focusing on writing – her dream since the age of nine. McHatton is the author of *Expressions of the Soul (2015), Stolen Moments (2015),* and *Into the Meadow (2015)* (written under her pen name Cristie Noll).

Raymond Neely, a proud native of southern West Virginia, is an influential Appalachian author, poet, writer and cannonist of

Appalachia. He is dedicated to writing "genuine" poetry of the region about the people, places, and ideas of the thriving communities. His poetry is published in *Appalachian Journal, The Bluestone Review*, and the *Pine Mountain Sand and Gravel* anthologies. Raymond Neely remains active in organizing and participating in local and regional literary arts societies, and aspires to bring about the further ascent of local arts, literature, artists, and poets.

Janet Ransom is one of five children raised in Shady Spring, West Virginia. She is the mother to one daughter and a granddaughter, and feels blessed to be Christian of the Baptist faith. Being hearing impaired, reading and writing have long been her media of choice.

Warren Reuschel is a freelance environmental consultant and writer. Although he was born in Maryland, he moved to Huntington at age four, and then to Beckley at age five. He grew up in Raleigh County and the nearby New River Gorge, with his parents and eight siblings. He graduated from Shady Spring High School and discovered a love for science and ecology at Marshall University, where he completed his Bachelor of Science and continued through Graduate School, researching stream and river restoration ecology. A short course in creative writing from John Van Kirk at Marshall gave him an alternative to the technical and scientific writing of his graduate work, and he has been writing short stories and poetry ever since. After nearly two decades of consulting throughout the Southeast, he now lives on a small farm along the Bluestone River in Mercer County with his wife and family.

Eva Smith-Carroll is a native of Raleigh County. She graduated from Marshall University and worked for West Virginia and Kentucky newspapers. Eva began a second career as an information officer for the Commonwealth of Kentucky and retired from state government in 2009. She collects West Virginia words and phrases and writes about her family history.

Linda Tabor was born and raised in Raleigh County, West Virginia, where she still resides. She and her husband, Paul, are, co-owners of a successful contracting business that was established in 1991. Linda enjoys relaxing with her guitar and traveling the state, taking photographs of the scenic landscapes that define the beauty that is West Virginia. She also loves the art of cooking, and takes pleasure in preparing meals for family and friends. Writing is one way she stays connected to parts of her life that would otherwise get lost in the ordinary routine of everyday living. She has been writing since the age of fourteen, when she realized words are a way to capture moments that may fade with the passage of time, just as one captures images in a photograph.

Tony Wegmann is a singer-songwriter from Kanawha County, West Virginia. He is currently writing songs and performing with his brother as a duo known as the Wegmann Brothers, and also as a solo artist. Most of his songs are related to West Virginia, its geography, its people, and its history. Returning to the state after a twenty-five year absence gave him a unique point of view, reflected in his multi-faceted creativity.

Simi Wilkins collects Appalachian lore and songs, and researches the rich and varied history of minorities in the region.

Joseph Wroz is descended from Hungarian immigrants into the southern West Virginia coalfields. He views it as his mission to revive both his family's eastern European and coalfield cultural traditions, which he feels were lost after his grandfather became part of the 1950s flight of underemployed miners to the northern industrial cities.

Special thanks to: Prolific South Carolina author **T. Allen Winn** served as a consultant to this work. His published fiction includes the *Detective Trudy Wagner* series, *Road Rage* and *North of the Border*; the bully book, *Dark Thirty*; the paranormal mystery *The Perfect Spook House*, and memoir *The Caregiver's Son*. His latest releases are memoir *Cornbread and Buttermilk, Good Old Fashioned Home Cooked Nostalgic Nonsense* and paranormal thriller *Lou Who*. He is a 'homegrown southerner" from the Palmetto State, presently residing on the South Carolina Grand Strand.

Ed note: A few of our contributors chose to not submit a biography, though their work speaks for them.

Made in the USA
Middletown, DE
27 April 2016